LIVES OF
THE SAINTS

Seven One-Act Plays

BY DAVID IVES

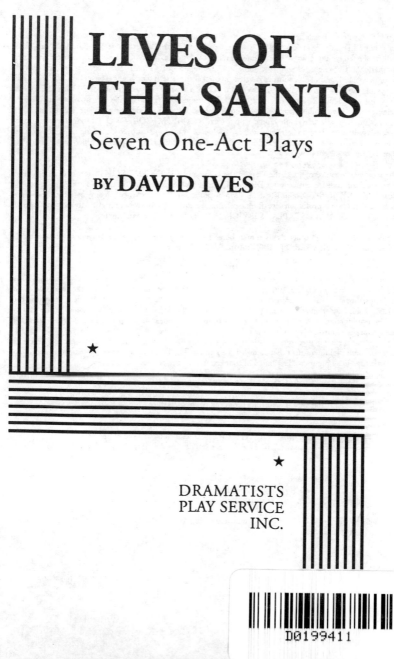

★

★

DRAMATISTS
PLAY SERVICE
INC.

*These plays are dedicated
to my mother,
Regina Roszkowski.*

Vivat! Vivat Regina!

The author thanks the Guggenheim Foundation,
whose generous support helped these plays get written.

TABLE OF CONTENTS

ENIGMA VARIATIONS

ENIGMA VARIATIONS premiered as part of an evening entitled *Lives of the Saints* at the Philadelphia Theatre Company (Sara Garonzik, Artistic Director) in January 1999. It was directed by John Rando; the set design was by Russell Metheny; the lighting design was by Robert Wierzel; the sound design was by Jim Van Bergin; and the costume design was by Kaye Voyce. The cast was as follows:

BEBE 1	Nancy Opel
BEBE 2	Anne O'Sullivan
BILL 1	Arnie Burton
BILL 2	Bradford Cover
FIFI	Danton Stone

ENIGMA VARIATIONS

Two identical chairs, side by side at center left, face two different chairs, identical to each other, side by side at center right. Upstage: two adjoining windows, looking out on exactly the same cityscape. A bell rings and lights come up on Bill 1 standing at far left, Bebe 1 at far right. Bill 1 wears a white lab coat and glasses, Bebe 1 an attractive but demure outfit.

BILL 1. Good morning, good morning. Ms. Doppelgängler?

BEBE 1. Actually, Mrs. Doppelgängler. Bebe W. Doppelgängler. With two small dots.

BILL 1. I'm Bill Williams. *(They cross to each other and shake hands, as Bill 2 and Bebe 2 enter just upstage of them and shake hands. Bill 2 and Bebe 2 wear exactly the same clothes as Bill 1 and Bebe 1 and make every move that their partners make, shadowing every gesture of Bill 1 and Bebe 1.)*

BEBE 1. Thank you so much for seeing me, Doctor.

BILL 1. Why don't you call me Bill.

BEBE 1. Bill.

BILL 1. Or Will.

BEBE 1. Will.

BILL 1. Will … you have a seat?

BEBE 1. Thank you. *(The two Bebe's sit and simultaneously adjust their skirts at their knees, as the two Bill's sit and in identical fashion adjust their identical glasses.)*

BILL 1. So. You have been having a problem.

BEBE 1. A couple of problems, you might say. But may we speak alone?

BILL 1. *(Looks behind himself.)* We are alone.

BEBE 1. *(Turns and looks over her shoulder.)* Where were we?

BILL 1. We were having a couple of problems.

BEBE 1. I'm not actually sure you're the right person to come to, Doctor. *(The Bills make a gesture and she corrects herself.)* Bill. — Will. — Well, you see, lately I've been having this funny feeling that there's more to the world than I thought. Or, think.
BILL 1. Could you ... expand a little?
BEBE 1. *(Takes a deep breath, expanding and contracting.)* It's as if, when I'm alone in a room, I'm somehow ... not alone. As if it's not just me there.
BILL 1. Mm-hm, mm-hm.
BEBE 1. And it's not just me. I mean — when I'm with someone it's almost as if there's one more than one of that someone in the room. And as if that one room isn't the only room I'm in. It's as if the world were somehow ... somehow ... double.
BILL 1. A singular problem, Mrs. Doppelgängler. But you're a singular person. Both of us know that. Two things: You're married?
BEBE 1. I'm single. We split up.
BILL 1. Any siblings?
BEBE 1. My twin sister, in St. Paul.
BILL 1. The twin city. How have you been sleeping?
BEBE 1. I'm up half the night in a double bed.
BILL 1. It doesn't add up.
BEBE 1. I'm desperate, Doctor. Last week I played doubles without a partner.
BILL 1. Did you win?
BEBE 1. Twice!
BILL 1. How did you manage that?
BEBE 1. Duplicity. Doublemint?
BILL 1. No thank you. Would you read the eye chart, please? *(Two identical eye charts fly in, side by side.)*
BEBE 1. Which one?
BILL 1. The one on the left.
BEBE 1. "E-I-E-I-O."
BILL 1. And on the right?
BEBE 1. "E-I-E-I-O."
BILL 1. Excellent. *(The eye charts fly back out.)*
BEBE 1. I know this sounds pretty odd.
BILL 1. Oh, we in my profession hear all kinds of O-D-D-D items.
BEBE 1. "O-D-D-D"...?

BILL 1. Odd. But I have news for you, Mrs. Doppelgängler: You are not alone.

BEBE 1. In what way?

BILL 1. In two ways. *(The Bills rise together and look out the two windows.)* Each person, which is to say everybody, looks out at the world and wonders, though apparently there's only one, if there aren't other worlds, and asks if there isn't more to it, or them, than they, that is he or she, think. Or thinks. Maybe, perhaps, there's possibly a higher reality. Or realities. Multiple realities, doing double duty. In any cases, I'm not just Bill W. Williams, and you're not just Bebe — Bebe? — Bebe W. Doppelgängler.

BEBE 1. Bebe W. W. Doppelgängler.

BILL 1. Exactly! And you alone can help yourself.

BEBE 1. If not me, then who?

BILL 1. *(Sitting.)* I stand corrected. The only alternatives ha ha ha! is that you're crazy. You're not crazy, are you?

BEBE 1. No. No.

BILL 1. Delusional? Mad?

BEBE 1. No …

BILL 1. Any — or many — multiple "personalities"?

BEBE 1. No. No. No. No. *(The Bebes take out identical handkerchiefs.)* It's as if I'm living some kind of double life. Am I ill, Will?

BILL 1. Well, I think we should see each other again. Possibly again and again. Maybe more than once. *(Presses intercom button in his chair arm.)* Fifi — would you come in here, please? *(Fifi enters, a hairy, burly guy in a nurse's white dress and shoes. He makes no attempt to seem "feminine" or "effeminate.")*

FIFI. Yes, doctor. You wanted me?

BILL 1. Bebe — Fifi. Fifi — Bebe. Mademoiselle LeBlanc is my temporary assistant.

FIFI. *Oui, oui.*

BEBE 1. Yes, we, we met.

BILL 1. Fifi, a wee matter. Would you set up a couple of appointments for Mrs. Doppelgängler?

FIFI. Two small dots?

BEBE 1. Two small dots.

BILL 1. I see your points. Same time all right?

BEBE 1. Fine, fine.

BILL 1. Fifi?

FIFI. Oui, oui. *(Fifi exits.)*

BILL 1. A wonderful woman. Dual citizenship. And exclusively bisexual.

BEBE 1. Doctor, can you suggest anything for me?

BILL 1. Maybe, Bebe — a double dose of B1 and B2 taken twice every couple of days for two weeks. As a one-time treatment. Are you covered?

BEBE 1. They pay half. Would you send me a bill, Bill?

BILL 1. In duplicate.

BEBE 1. *(Rising.)* Thank you so, so much.

BILL 1. You're very, very welcome. *(Bill 1 and Bebe 1 shake hands, Bill 2 and Bebe 2 shake hands. As they do so, they freeze and we hear a bell ring. The scene in the windows changes to a different cityscape.)*

BILL 2. Good morning, good morning. Ms. Doppelgängler.

BEBE 2. Actually, Mrs. Doppelgängler. Bebe W. W. Doppelgängler.

BILL 2. Two small dots.

BEBE 2. That's right. Thank you so much for seeing me.

BILL 2. Will you have a seat? *(The four sit exactly as before.)* So. You've been having a recurring problem.

BEBE 2. I have, Doctor.

BILL 2. I *am* Doctor, but you can call me Bill.

BEBE 2. Bill.

BILL 2. Or Will.

BEBE 2. Will.

BILL 2. Well?

BEBE 2. Well, I'm not sure you're the right person to come to, but you see I keep having this feeling … I keep having this feeling I've been through all this before.

BILL 2. Could you expand a little?

BEBE 2. *(Takes a deep breath, expanding and contracting.)* I feel as if I've been through all this before. It's as if this isn't the first time this has happened to me.

BILL 2. Have we ever been through this before?

BEBE 2. Never.

BILL 2. Have you felt this way often?

BEBE 2. This isn't the first time.

BILL 2. Do your meals repeat on you?

BEBE 2. Again and again. I reiterate.

BILL 2. You reiterate what?

BEBE 2. Nothing, I just keep reiterating.

BILL 2. So your recurring problem is a *recurring* problem.

BEBE 2. Frequently. I even bought a repeating pistol.

BILL 2. Repeating...?

BEBE 2. Repeating pistol.

BILL 2. Will you continue?

BEBE 2. I certainly hope so.

BILL 2. No, I mean — please continue.

BEBE 2. I'm not sure you're the right person to come to, but you see I keep having this feeling ... I keep having this feeling I've been through this before.

BILL 2. Could you expand a little?

BEBE 2. *(Takes a deep breath, expanding and contracting.)* I feel as if I've been through all this before. It's as if this isn't the first time this has happened to me.

BILL 2. Have we ever been through this before?

BEBE 2. Never.

BILL 2. Have you felt this way often?

BEBE 2. This isn't the first time.

BILL 2. Do your meals repeat on you?

BEBE 2. Again and again. I reiterate.

BILL 2. You reiterate what?

BEBE 2. Nothing, I just keep reiterating.

BILL 2. So your recurring problem is a *recurring* problem.

BEBE 2. Frequently. I even bought a repeating pistol.

BILL 2. Repeating...?

BEBE 2. Repeating pistol.

BILL 2. Will you continue?

BEBE 2. I certainly hope so.

BILL 2. No, I mean — please continue.

BEBE 2. I'm not sure you're the right person to come to, Doctor —

BILL 2. Let me say one word. A word I'm sure you've heard before, Mrs. Doppelgängler.

BEBE 2. *(Pronounced with a silly, tight "ü.")* Déja vuuu?

BILL 2. *Déja vuuu.*

BEBE 2. So it's ... *déja vuuu?*

13

BILL 2. *Déja vuuu.* I repeat.

BEBE 2. *Déja vuuu?*

BILL 2. *Déja vuuu.* Mrs. Doppelgängler, you have a German name but a French disease. I call that serious.

BEBE 2. Well this isn't something I haven't heard before. *Déja vuuu?*

BILL 2. *Déja vuuu.*

BEBE 2. But this time it really means something.

BILL 2. Ditto.

BEBE 2. But Doctor, what can I, what can I duuu — about *déja vuuu?*

BILL 2. I think we should see each other again. Possibly again and again. Maybe more than once.

BEBE 2. *(Rising.)* Thank you so much, Will.

BILL 2. So — come again?

BEBE 2. I said thank you so much, Will.

BILL 2. I mean will you come again.

BEBE 2. I said thank you so much, Will.

BILL 2. No, I mean, will you come here one more time?

BEBE 2. I'd love to.

BILL 2. Just one more time?

BEBE 2. I said I'd love to.

BILL 2. No, I mean will you come...?

BEBE 2. I will, Will.

BILL 2. One more time or many more times?

BEBE 2. How about next week?

BILL 2. Let's re-confirm. Fifi? *(Fifi enters.)*

FIFI. Oui, oui, Doctor.

BILL 2. Repeat the usual. *(Fifi exits. Bill 1 shakes hands with Bebe 2 and Bill 2 shakes hands with Bebe 1, and they freeze a moment as a bell rings. The windows change to two totally different scenes.)*

BEBE 1. *(Bebe 2 gestures as if she's speaking, while Bebe 1, remaining very still, speaks for her.)* Good morning, good morning. How are you, Bill?

BILL 1. *(Bill 2 gestures as if he's speaking, while Bill 1, remaining very still, speaks for him.)* Thank you for seeing me, Dr. Doppelgängler.

BEBE 2. *(Gestures as before.)*   BEBE 1. That's what we're here

14

BEBE 1. ... for. And please, call me Bebe. Won't you have a seat?

BILL 2. *(Gestures as before.)*

BILL 1. Thank you. *(The four sit.)*

BEBE 2. *(Gestures as before.)*

BEBE 1. Apparently you seem to be having a possible problem.

BILL 2. *(Gestures as before.)*

BILL 1. Apparently I seem to be having a possible problem. Exactly!

BEBE 2. *(Gestures.)*

BEBE 1. Could you amplify a little?

BILL 2. *(Gestures.)*

BILL 1. *(Very loudly.)* I DON'T KNOW IF YOU'RE THE RIGHT PERSON TO COME TO ...

BEBE 2. *(Gestures.)*

BEBE 1. I mean, could you expand a little.

BILL 2. *(Gestures.)*

BILL 1. I don't know if you're the right person, Doctor ... *(Bebe 2 gestures and he corrects himself.)* ... Bebe ... But I am tormented lately by this feeling that everything — everything around us — everything in the world is just an illusion.

BEBE 2. *(Gestures.)*

BEBE 1. Really?

BILL 2. *(Gestures.)*

BILL 1. It's all a fantasy. A figment. A facade. A phantasm. A false front. A *fata morgana*. And frankly it frightens me.

BEBE 2. *(Gestures.)*

BEBE 1. Fascinating. Would you read the eye chart, please? *(Bebe 2 gestures to empty space: NO EYE CHART FLIES IN.)*

BILL 2. *(Gestures.)*

BILL 1. Which one?

BEBE 2. *(Gestures.)*

BEBE 1. The one on the left.

BILL 2. *(Gestures.)*

BILL 1. *(Babbles incoherently as if in deadly fear.)*

BEBE 2. *(Gestures.)*

BEBE 1. Good. Now read line two.

BILL 2. *(Gestures.)*

BILL 1. *(Babbles incoherently.)*

15

BEBE 2. *(Gestures.)*

BILL 2. *(Gestures.)*

BEBE 2. *(Gestures.)*

BILL 2. *(Gestures.)*

BEBE 2. *(Gestures.)*

BILL 2. *(Gestures.)*

BEBE 2. *(Gestures.)*

BILL 2. *(Gestures.)*

BEBE 2. *(Gestures.)*

BILL 2. *(Gestures.)*

BEBE 2. *(Gestures.)*

BILL 2. *(Gestures.)*

BEBE 2. *(Gestures.)*

BEBE 1. Very good. And the eye chart on the right?

BILL 1. There is no chart on the right.

BEBE 1. Excellent.

BILL 1. Doctor, this feeling follows me wherever I go. Or seem to go. It's as if, whatever I'm seeing, or whatever I seem to be seeing, isn't what's really there.

BEBE 1. I see.

BILL 1. As if all this is just … a charade. Or a game. Or a veil. *(Takes a veil out of his pocket. Terrified:)* This is a veil! Isn't it?

BEBE 1. Do you see a veil?

BILL 1. *(Puts veil away.)* Never mind. Maybe I'm not talking to you. Maybe I'm not talking to *you.* Maybe I'm not the one who's not even talking to someone who's not even you.

BEBE 1. Talk to me, Bill.

BILL 1. Is all this actually nothing with something else behind it, or is it something with nothing behind it?

BEBE 1. *(Has no idea what he's talking about.)* Uhhhhhhhhhhhhh- hhhhhhh …

BILL 1. Maybe I don't even have a problem. Maybe I only think I have a problem. Doctor, what do you think you think?

BEBE 1. Well. I think … *(We hear a fast version of "Pop Goes the Weasel" as the four circle the chairs. The music stops and they all stop.)*

BEBE 1. I think we're making progress. *(The music continues and again they run around the chairs. Fifi enters and blows a gym coach whistle and the four freeze in position as the music stops. Windows change to the scenes they had at the beginning.)*

FIFI. *(To us.)* In the great dance of life, the possible positions are so many, the organs are so few. Some years ago, a scientist floated a man face down in a deep pool. The man in the pool wore a pair of special goggles that blanked out his vision into a field of pure and limitless white. After several hours the man began to hallucinate. He thought he was walking down a street in Paris. In a fictive cafe near the Eiffel Tower he hallucinated a beautiful woman and immediately fell in love with her. I, Fifi LeBlanc, was that woman. But am I really Fifi LeBlanc, former *au pair* — or am I Aphrodite, the eternal goddess of love? Or am I, as I have begun to suspect, Franklin Spong, a gym teacher from Kankakee, wearing a dress? And how does this affect my health insurance? The need for meaning! The search for answers! The great question! Class, what is the question?

BILLS and BEBES. Help!

FIFI. Correct. Everybody into the pool! *(Fifi blows the whistle. Blackout.)*

PROPERTY LIST

Veil (BILL)
Gym-coach whistle (FIFI)

SOUND EFFECTS

Bell ringing
Fast version of "Pop Goes the Weasel"

THE MYSTERY AT TWICKNAM VICARAGE

THE MYSTERY AT TWICKNAM VICARAGE was first presented as a part of a revised *Lives of the Saints* at the Berkshire Theatre Festival (Kate Maguire, Artistic Director) in August 1999. It was directed by John Rando; the set design was by Russell Metheny; the lighting design was by Robert Wierzel; the sound design was by Jim Van Bergin; and the costume design was by Kaye Voyce. The cast was as follows:

SARAH .... Nancy Opel
INSPECTOR .... Danton Stone
MONA .... Anne O'Sullivan
ROGER .... Arnie Burton
JEREMY .... Stephen DeRosa

THE MYSTERY AT TWICKNAM VICARAGE

In the dark before curtain: A grandfather clock chimes seven times. Then we hear three pistol shots. A woman (Sarah) screams. Lights come up on Jeremy Thumpington-Fffienes — that's pronounced "Fuh-Fuh-Fines" — lying dead on a rug at center with a drinks glass in his hand. Inspector Dexter, in a trenchcoat, is kneeling over the body. Around them are Mona Thumpington-Fffienes, the Rev. Roger Penworthy-Pilks, Sarah Penworthy-Pilks, and a couch. Masterpiece Theatre accents.

SARAH. Good Lord. Is he…? Is he…? Is he…?

DEXTER. Dead?

SARAH. Is he dead?

DEXTER. Yes, 'e's dead. Mr. Jeremy Thumpington-Fuh-Fuh-Fines 'as been shot three times through the heart. Probably within this very room, probably on this very carpet. Very nice carpet, by the way.

SARAH. Thank you, Inspector.

ROGER. *(Very plummy accent.)* I'm syorry, Inspyector Dexter. Did you say Jeremy is … Jeremy is … Jeremy is dyead?

DEXTER. 'is ventricles 'ave been completely ventilated, sir.

MONA. And yet such a brief short while ago Jerry was so alive, he was so terribly, terribly alive.

SARAH. Certainly changes our dinner plans.

ROGER. *(Pronounces "shooting" to rhyme with "footing.")* I presume this was a shuuting ekcident, Inspyector Dexter?

DEXTER. A what?

ROGER. A shuuting ekcident.

DEXTER. Oh, "shuuting ekcident." No, Rector, this was no mere shuuting ekcident.

SARAH. But you don't mean that it was…? It was…? It was…?

DEXTER. Murder?

SARAH. Muhdeh?

DEXTER. Yes. It was murder.

ROGER, SARAH and MONA. *(Sharp, horrified intake of breath.)*

ROGER. Muhdeh…?

MONA. Muhdeh…?

SARAH. Muhdeh…?

DEXTER. And I believe it was somebody in this very room who murdered him.

ROGER, SARAH and MONA. *(Sharp, horrified intake of breath.)*

MONA. In this room?

ROGER. In this room?

SARAH. In this — ?

DEXTER. *(Cutting her off.)* I think that's enough of that. Was it you who killed him, Reverend Roger Penworthy-Pilks, the Rector of Twicknam?

ROGER. I? How dyare you insinuate such a thing! You might say I … I … I loved the man, dyemmit, in some … squishy way.

DEXTER. Was it you who killed him, Mrs. Reverend Sarah Penworthy-Pilks?

SARAH. It was not I, for your information, Inspector Dexter.

DEXTER. You're quite a cool, as the Americans say, cucumber. Or did you, the man's own wife do it, Mona Thumpington-Fuh-Fuh-Fuh-Fuh-Fines?

MONA. Only two "Fuh's" in "Fuh-Fuh-Fines."

DEXTER. Sorry.

MONA. *(Immediately hysterical.)* No, I didn't kill him! I swear it! Yes, yes, I wanted him dead sometimes. I planned to murder him every now and again, often on Tuesdays for some reason, I even bought a rare Pakistani poison and a set of pinking shears that might've seemed an accident. But no I didn't kill him! I'm innocent! I swear it by all that's holy!

DEXTER. Protesting a bit much, if you ask me. Well, one of you did it and I'm going to find out who.

SARAH. I suggest you question Mona.

MONA. I suggest you question Sarah.

DEXTER. Rector?

ROGER. I suggest you question them too.

MONA. I always envied you, Sarah. I confess it. Your beauty. Your coolness. Your beautiful bottom. Your thrilling long, long legs. Your beautiful bottom. Did I say beautiful bottom already? Your Wedgewood. Your tea cozies.

SARAH. And my husband.

MONA. And your husband.

SARAH. You slept with him, didn't you?

MONA. Only once, but it wasn't successful!

SARAH. I was speaking to Roger, thank you. You slept with Jeremy, didn't you?

ROGER. Only twice, and it wasn't ... very successful.

SARAH. Well I've slept with you twice and I can believe that. And I slept with Jeremy three times and we were very successful.

ROGER. Viper.

SARAH. Amphibian. *(They stick their tongues out at each other.)*

DEXTER. Rector.

ROGER. Inspector?

DEXTER. Jeremy Thumpington-Fuh-Fuh-Fines was quite sexually active, was he not?

ROGER. Inspector, the man was insatiable. I once came in here and thought he was sleeping on the sofa, actually he was sleeping *with* the sofa. The liaison went on for some months, until he chucked the sofa for my green leather wingchair.

DEXTER. You're not suggesting the sofa might've shot him — ?

ROGER. I suggest you question the sofa. Maybe then you'll find the trooth.

DEXTER. The what?

ROGER. The trooth. You know. The fyects.

DEXTER. The what?

ROGER. The fyects.

DEXTER. Ah, the "fyects." Yes, I demand the fyects about what happened here tonight!

MONA. Oh, who cares who killed Jerry! He's dead, isn't he? That's all that's important, isn't it? That he's gone to glory? Passed over? Gone west? Put out to sea? Kicked the bucket? Cashed in, popped off, pegged out, curled up his toes, slipped his cable, croaked on the carpet during cocktails? Isn't that what's important?

Well … not under the circumstances, I suppose …

DEXTER. Rector.

ROGER. Yes, Inspector.

DEXTER. Was there any tension in the room prior to Mr. Thumpington-Fuh-Fuh-Fines's death?

ROGER. Tension? Was there tension, darling?

SARAH. Tension?

ROGER. Let me think backwards … *(Lights change as Roger, Sarah, and Mona walk backwards as if into flashback. Jeremy springs to his feet, drinks glass in hand. He's got three bright red bullet holes in his shirt front. Inspector Dexter remains, and observes.)*

JEREMY. *(Wobbling drunk.)* Well isn't this is a bloody boring party.

MONA. Stop it, Jerry, stop it! You're drunk!

SARAH. *(Throws a drink in Jeremy's face.)* Damn you, Jeremy! Damn you!

ROGER. *(Throws his drink in Jeremy's face.)* Sir, you're a cad! *(All freeze. Speaking to the Inspector.)* There may have been a little tension in the room. *(All un-freeze.)*

MONA. But I say, let's not quarrel, shall we?

SARAH. Hellish weather, isn't it?

ROGER. I've never seen such snyow.

MONA. I find it so comforting. Snyow …

JEREMY. Bollocks.

ROGER. Who needs a drinkie? Whiskey soda, Mona?

MONA. Love one, Roger-Dodger.

SARAH. It's now three minutes to the hour. Dinner's ready when the clock strikes seven.

MONA and ROGER. Huzzah!

MONA. I hope you made the cheese things. I do love the cheese things.

ROGER. The cheese things are scrumptious, are they not.

JEREMY. Bollocks.

ROGER. We found a wonderful *restaurong* — *(Bad French pronunciation.)* — by the by. Antarctican cuisine.

MONA. Antarctican?

ROGER. Roasted penguin. Tastes a lot like nun, actually. Hahahahaha.

MONA. Like nun? Oh, yes! Penguin, like nun. Hahahahaha.

ROGER. We ate — and then there were nun.

ROGER, SARAH and MONA. Hahahahaha.

JEREMY. Bollocks.

SARAH. Have we all seen Prime Suspect Fifteen?

MONA. It's not nearly as good as Twelve.

JEREMY. Bollocks. My God, we're not going to sit about and make bloody small talk all evening, are we? Talk about the weather and restaurants and what we've seen on the fucking telly? Might as well critique the shape and consistency of human turds as talk about what's good on the fucking telly.

MONA. *(Weepy.)* Spoil sport. Sad sack. Gloomy boots. Party pooper.

JEREMY. You know we're all going to croak someday. *(All freeze.)*

SARAH. *(Out front, spookily.)* It was almost as if he'd had a pre-monition about his own death. *(All un-freeze.)*

JEREMY. I could be a corpse on this carpet in a moment — beautiful carpet, by the way — and I'm supposed to discuss the bloody cheese things?

MONA. Stop it, Jerry, stop it, stop it! I hate it when you get morbid like this!

JEREMY. My God, does none of us read? Does none of us think?

ROGER, SARAH and MONA. *(Variously, ad lib.)* Well, not really … No, I wouldn't say so … I don't, myself …

JEREMY. Does none of us have anything at all of substance to say?

ROGER. Well I don't much believe much in God much, anymore.

SARAH. Roger …

ROGER. Just making conversation, darling.

JEREMY. Look at us. None of us is living a life worth living. We're pathetic toothy boring creatures with ridiculous accents.

SARAH. *(Toothily.)* "Toothy"?

ROGER. Ekcents? What ekcents?

JEREMY. We're a lot of rotting corpses is what we are. Isn't that the terrible horrible awful truth?

MONA. Stop it, Jerry, stop it! You're drunk!

SARAH. *(Throwing her drink in Jeremy's face.)* Damn you, Jeremy! Damn you!

ROGER. *(Throwing his drink in Jeremy's face.)* Sir, you're a cad!

(Clock strikes.)

SARAH. Just then, the clock started to strike.

MONA. The lights went out. *(Lights go to half.)*

ROGER. Good God, what's happened to the lights?

SARAH. And on the final stroke of seven … *(We hear three shots. Jeremy falls to the floor.)* Bang, bang, bang. Three shots. Probably from a Webley .45 — just a guess. Then somebody screamed. I think it may have been me. *(Screams.)* Yes, it was me. And when the lights came up. *(Lights back up to full.)* Jeremy was lying in missionary position on my carpet. He'd had an affair with that carpet, so at first I thought they were copulating.

MONA. I can't believe that such a brief short while ago he was so alive, he was so terribly, terribly alive … I'm sorry, did I say that already?

DEXTER. If what you say is true, Mrs. Penworthy-Pilks, then the murder weapon is still in this room.

ROGER, SARAH and MONA. *(Horrified intake of breath.)*

DEXTER. Indeed, the fatal pistol is still in someone's pocket. *(All three reach for their pockets and look about suspiciously.)* It's not as if any of you lacked motive. Why, even the furniture wanted him dead.

MONA. But we didn't want him dead. We loved Jeremy. He was so charming, so fun, so …

SARAH. Priapic.

MONA. So priapic. What's priapic? *(Sarah shows the size of Jeremy's sexual endowment with her hands spaced apart.)* So priapic.

DEXTER. Well I'm going to have the truth. Excuse me. The trooth.

ROGER. Inspector.

DEXTER. Rector?

ROGER. I have a confession to make.

DEXTER. Sort of your job, isn't it?

ROGER. I mean I have to make a confession to you.

DEXTER. What sort of confession?

ROGER. Well, I don't much believe much in God much anymore …

DEXTER. Is that your confession?

ROGER. No, that's not my confession.

DEXTER. Sorry.

ROGER. Anyway, now that I'm confessing I might as well say I don't really like the cheese things very much either.

SARAH. You don't like the cheese things?

ROGER. I can say that now. I never much liked the cheese things very much, though I always said they were scrumptious. The trooth of it is, I was lying.

SARAH. *(Tragically.)* I always sensed that you didn't like the cheese things.

MONA. I've always loved the cheese things.

DEXTER. Must we discuss the bloody cheese things?

MONA. Jerry said exactly the same thing, right before he was riddled with hot lead.

ROGER. In any case, Inspector, you can take me away — for it was I who ventilated Jeremy's ventricles.

SARAH, MONA and DEXTER. *(Horrified intake of breath.)*

ROGER. *(Taking out a small pistol.)* With this starting pistol.

SARAH, MONA and DEXTER. *(Horrified intake of breath.)*

ROGER. Which I stole from my public school when I was twelve.

SARAH, MONA and DEXTER. *(Horrified intake of breath.)*

ROGER. It's very hard to say all this as a disbelieving Christian because now I'm going to be hanged and I'll go into eternal empty void nothingness forever and ever instead of paradise — a nice place I always pictured rather like Brighton but without the tourists. Anyway I loved Jerry in some … squishy way … Did I say that already? But I couldn't stand it when he threw me over for the sofa, especially since I so badly desired that sofa myself.

DEXTER. Thank you, Rector.

ROGER. It is so nice and fluffy. I'd even fondled it on a couple of occasions when Sarah wasn't around.

DEXTER. Thank you, Rector.

ROGER. Then when I found Jeremy'd had my green leather wingchair it was too, too much. My God, he had a passion for things!

DEXTER. Certainly left his mark on them, didn't he.

ROGER. *(Weeping on Dexter's shoulder.)* I'm sorry. I'm sorry.

DEXTER. Very well, sir. Now if you'll follow me to the Yard …

ROGER. The yard? What's out in the yard?

DEXTER. *Scotland* Yard.

ROGER. Oh, Scotland Yard. Yes. That.

SARAH. Just one moment, Inspector. As a partially disbelieving Christian I cannot allow this to happen. It was not only Roger with the starting pistol who killed Jeremy, it was I — with this Webley .45. *(Lifts skirt and shows a gun strapped to her leg. Dexter whistles, Mona howls, and Roger barks like a dog.)* Thank you. Anyway I'm willing to face my Maker — if there really is one. My true punishment is to've killed the only man I ever loved.

ROGER. The only man — ? Really, darling?

SARAH. Let me finish. The only man I ever loved in a hammock. I shall miss that hammock. You can take us away now.

MONA. Stop, Inspector! It was not only Sarah with the Webley and Roger with the starting pistol. It was I, with this .505 telescopic elephant hunting rifle. *(She takes an enormous hunting rifle from behind the couch.)* I shot him in conspiracy with the sofa, who hid the weapon for me. I don't need to tell you why I killed him. It was the sardine sandwiches he had for breakfast.

ROGER, SARAH and DEXTER. Eeeuw.

MONA. Now how I shall miss his oily little fishes.

ROGER. I shall miss his happy hedonistic laughter.

SARAH. I shall miss tickling his testicles while he sang the Oxford boating song.

DEXTER. You'll all miss him, but you all *shot* him, didn't you?

ROGER, SARAH and MONA. *(Variously, ad lib.)* Yes, well, there is that ... It's true ... You do have a point ... *(Jeremy jumps to his feet.)*

JEREMY. I say, chaps, is dinner on yet?

MONA. Jerry!

SARAH. Jerry!

ROGER. Jerry!

DEXTER. Jerry!

JEREMY. I'm sorry. Was I copulating with the rug again? Oh dear, I say, I seem to've been shot.

ROGER. Yes, Jerry, I'm afraid there's been a bit of a ... shuuting ekcident.

JEREMY. A what?

ROGER. A shuuting ekcident.

JEREMY. Oh, a shuuting ekcident. Well the bullets seem to've ventilated but not violated my ventricles. *(To Dexter:)* Who're you?

DEXTER. 'arry Dexter of the Yard, sir.

JEREMY. I say, haven't we slept together?

DEXTER. That would be two years ago last April, sir.

JEREMY. Oh, yes. The butterscotch pudding.

DEXTER. Quite right, sir. I cherish the memory.

JEREMY. Aren't you sweet.

DEXTER. But if you're not dead, sir, I have to say my purpose in life is quite evaporated. *(Weeps.)* I've been rendered redundant. I'm 'aving existential doubts, sir! What ever shall I do with my dwindling empty days?

JEREMY. You might try gardening and get in touch with the earth.

DEXTER. *(Stops weeping.)* An excellent idea, sir. I shall take up the spade.

JEREMY. In any case, chaps, I apologize for being so utterly beastly before the ... um ...

ROGER. Shuuting.

JEREMY. Shuuting ekcident. All that rot about death, and corpses. But you see some weeks ago my doctor told me I had this ... had this ... had this ingrown toenail.

ROGER. No.

SARAH. No.

MONA. No.

JEREMY. Yes, very serious. And I'd quite given up on life, you see. The bally thing made me so damned bitter and nihilistic.

MONA. Jerry, you never told me about your toenail!

JEREMY. I wanted to spare you, darling. The funny thing is, as I was lying there ventilated on the carpet I actually crossed over to the other side and I saw God, you see.

SARAH. You saw God?

JEREMY. In paradise. Quite rum, isn't it?

ROGER. So there is a God?

JEREMY. Nice chap. We had a wonderful chat about Prime Suspect Fifteen.

SARAH. Did God like Prime Suspect Fifteen?

JEREMY. God preferred Eleven.

SARAH. My theological doubts are dissipated!

JEREMY. God also suggested I start appreciating the beauty of things and stop copulating with them.

MONA. What was paradise like?

JEREMY. Nice place. Rather like Brighton without the tourists. In any case I lost all my bitterness and I realized that this world is quite nice, really. And then I woke up and I loved it all. I loved the snow — so comforting — and I even loved the cheese things.

SARAH. Roger says he doesn't like the cheese things.

JEREMY. God told me he adores the cheese things.

ROGER. God adores the cheese things?

JEREMY. Even the cheese things are part of God.

ROGER. Then I shall love the cheese things with all my heart!

JEREMY. Mostly I realize now how much I love you all — well I *have* loved you all, haven't I, in quite a variety of ways. I mean the hammock was brilliant!

SARAH. Dear, darling Jerry.

MONA. You're so alive again. You're so terribly, terribly alive.

DEXTER. Looks like we've got the trooth now, don't we, rector.

ROGER. Indeed we do, inspector. And God bless us, every one!

JEREMY. Anyone for sex?

ALL. Cheers! *(Blackout.)*

PROPERTY LIST

Drinks
Pistols (ROGER, SARAH)
Rifle (MONA)

SOUND EFFECTS

Grandfather clock chimes seven times
Pistol shots

BABEL'S IN ARMS

BABEL'S IN ARMS premiered as part of an evening entitled *Lives of the Saints* at the Philadelphia Theatre Company (Sara Garonzik, Artistic Director) in January 1999. It was directed by John Rando; the set design was by Russell Metheny; the lighting design was by Robert Wierzel; the sound design was by Jim Van Bergin; and the costume design was by Kaye Voyce. The cast was as follows:

GORPH .... Danton Stone
CANNAPFLIT .... Arnie Burton
EUNUCH .... Bradford Cover
PRIESTESS .... Anne O'Sullivan
BUSINESSWOMAN .... Nancy Opel

BABEL'S IN ARMS

Bare stage but for a palm tree and a sense of expansive blue sky overhead. a road sign with arrows points in various directions: "Nineveh 75 mi.," "Egypt 1,324 mi." and "Eden 6 mi.," which has been crossed out. Middle Eastern music. Enter two workers, Gorph and Cannapflit. They wear, respectively, blue and red belted tunics à la 1000 BC. Primitive tools hang from their belts, and a crowbar from Gorph's belt. They are carrying between them an enormous rectangular building stone, maybe five feet long and two feet high. They inch slowly toward center with it, as ...

GORPH. *(Groaning under the stone's weight.)* Okay ... Okay ... Okay ...

CANNAPFLIT. Okay?

GORPH. Okay.

CANNAPFLIT. Okay?

GORPH. Okay. Okay. Okay. Okay. Stop. *(A moment, as they catch their breath.)*

CANNAPFLIT. Okay?

GORPH. Go.

BOTH. *(Ad lib, moving toward center.)* Okay. Okay. Okay. Okay. Okay. Okay. Okay. Okay. Okay. Okay.

GORPH. Stop. *(They catch their breath a moment.)* Go. *(They move a few inches.)* Stop. *(They stop to catch their breath, but this time they insouciantly hold the stone with just a finger or two, making it obvious it's just a styrofoam prop.)* Go. *(Immediately:)* Stop. *(A moment.)* Go.

CANNAPFLIT. *(At center now.)* Stop.

GORPH. Okay. Down. *(They slowly lower the stone.)* Down. Down. Down. Down. Down. Stop. *(Looks at it.)* Behold. The fucker is backwards. *(They go in a circle.)* Circle.

CANNAPFLIT. Circle.

GORPH. Circle.

CANNAPFLIT. Circle.

GORPH. Circle.

CANNAPFLIT. Circle.

GORPH. Stop. *(The back looks just like the front. They check position.)* It was right the first way. Circle. *(They circle back the other way.)*

CANNAPFLIT. Circle.

GORPH. Circle.

CANNAPFLIT. Circle.

GORPH. Circle.

CANNAPFLIT. Circle.

GORPH. Circle. Stop. *(A moment.)*

CANNAPFLIT. Okay?

GORPH. Okay. Down.

CANNAPFLIT. Down.

GORPH. Down.

CANNAPFLIT. Down.

GORPH. Up.

CANNAPFLIT. Down.

GORPH. Up, up.

CANNAPFLIT. Up.

GORPH. Up.

CANNAPFLIT. Up. *(A pause.)*

GORPH. Down ... Down ... Down ... Down ... Stop. *(They now have it an inch over the ground.)* One. Two. Five. Go! *(They drop the stone to the ground.)* Behold the stone.

CANNAPFLIT. Behold the stone!

BOTH. Yes! *(They snort, they high-five, they shake hands, they flex their muscles, they grab crotch, and generally male-display.)*

GORPH. Heavy.

CANNAPFLIT. Heavy. *(They moan, they groan, they stretch, they wipe sweat from their foreheads.)*

GORPH. Heavy stone.

CANNAPFLIT. Heavy stone.

GORPH. Big stone.

CANNAPFLIT. Big stone. *(They moan, they groan, they stretch, they wipe sweat from each other's foreheads.)* But what is a "stone," O Gorph son of Khlekhmalekhm?

GORPH. That heavy fucker there. That is a stone, O Cannapflit son of Bob.

CANNAPFLIT. Ah, so that is a stone.

GORPH. Behold the stone!

CANNAPFLIT. Behold the stone! But are all similar fuckers whatever their size or color called a "stone"?

GORPH. Any fucker made of stone is called a "stone."

CANNAPFLIT. But is this stone in the right place, O Gorph son of Khlekhmalekhm?

GORPH. I will consult the plans, O Cannapflit son of Bob. *(He takes out a large parchment roll.)* Behold the plans.

CANNAPFLIT. Behold the plans! *(Gorph unrolls a blueprint — a large blue sheet of paper with just a single white rectangle in the middle.)*

GORPH. It looks close to me. Check the horizon.

CANNAPFLIT. Check the horizon. *(Cannapflit pats his pockets.)* What's a horizon?

GORPH. *(Pointing over audience.)* Behold the horizon.

CANNAPFLIT. Behold the horizon! *(Cannapflit puts up his hands to his eyes as if he were holding binoculars and scans the horizon.)*

GORPH. But why do you hold your hands in that silly-ass way, O son of Bob?

CANNAPFLIT. Because binoculars have not been invented yet.

GORPH. And what do you see on the horizon?

CANNAPFLIT. I see nothing.

GORPH. Not Nineveh?

CANNAPFLIT. Negative.

GORPH. Accad?

CANNAPFLIT. Eh-eh.

GORPH. Sodom?

CANNAPFLIT. Nada'm.

GORPH. Rehoboth-Ur?

CANNAPFLIT. No thur.

GORPH. The stone must move one sixteenth of an ell to the north!

CANNAPFLIT. One sixteenth of an ell! How far is that?

GORPH. About an inch.

CANNAPFLIT. *(As Gorph takes out the crowbar.)* What is that fucker, O my friend?

GORPH. This fucker has no name, for humanity is young and has not words yet for every fucker. Basically it's a rigid rod that pivots about a fulcrum and is used to move a fucker at point A by applying force at point B.

CANNAPFLIT. Oh.

GORPH. I call it a lever.

CANNAPFLIT. Oh, so that's a lever.

GORPH. Behold young levers wherever you are.

CANNAPFLIT. Behold the lever!

GORPH. I think humanity's had enough of that locution.

CANNAPFLIT. I will can it.

GORPH. Can it, O Cannapflit. *(With a huge moan of effort, he levers the stone an inch to the left; that done, he checks, and nudges it with his toe one last small bit.)* The stone is now in place.

CANNAPFLIT. The stone is in place! *(They snort, high-five, shake hands, flex muscles, grab crotch, and generally male-display.)* So what is the stone for, O Gorph?

GORPH. This stone? This stone is for … I do not know. You mean thou dost not know?

CANNAPFLIT. I dost not know. *(They regard the stone a moment.)*

GORPH. Dost-belt development — ?

CANNAPFLIT. Maybe condos. *(A eunuch/slave enters.)*

EUNUCH/SLAVE. *(Very high falsetto.)* Make way! Make way for the high priestess of Shinar!

GORPH. Eunuch?

CANNAPFLIT. Eunuch. *(The eunuch/slave blows a toy trumpet, leading a procession: a businesswoman in a killer suit with a large sword in a scabbard, and a priestess in outrageous outfit and very high platform shoes, who makes curious gestures. The businesswoman sets up a sign: "FUTURE HOME OF BABEL.")*

GORPH. Did I say development? "Future home of Baybel."

BUSINESSWOMAN. Babble.

GORPH. Excuse me?

BUSINESSWOMAN. It's not "Baybel." It's Babble.

GORPH. Oh. Babble not Baybel.

CANNAPFLIT. I can't even read, but it's spelled "Baybel."

BUSINESSWOMAN. Well it's Babble — rabble.

CANNAPFLIT. Okay, fine.

GORPH. The birth of the class structure. You were there.

PRIESTESS. *(Blessing the stone.)* Oh wow. Oh wow. Oh wow.
Oh wow.

CANNAPFLIT. High priestess?

GORPH. Sure looks high to me.

PRIESTESS. In the name of Nimrod, omnipotent and immortal
king of the land of Shinar!

EUNUCH/SLAVE. *(Bringing a potato on a velvet cushion;
falsetto.)* Behold the sacred potato!

GORPH and CANNAPFLIT. *(Falsetto, mocking him.)* Behold the
sacred potato!

EUNUCH/SLAVE. *(Aside to them, not in falsetto.)* Eat me, okay?
This is my *job*.

PRIESTESS. *(Taking potato and shaking it over the stone.)* In the
name of the sacred potato, I hereby consecrate this tower …
(Realizes it's only a stone.) I consecrate this future tower of Baybel
… Is it "Baybel" or "Babble"?

BUSINESSWOMAN. Babble.

PRIESTESS. It's spelled like Baybel.

BUSINESSWOMAN. The CEO says "Babble."

PRIESTESS. Okay, so … *(Shakes sacred potato again.)* … Babble
… district of Ammalekhkh, county of Cush, state of blah blah
blah, to the greater power and glory of our mighty king Nimrod
and his wife Debbie. All say "Oh wow."

ALL. Oh wow.

PRIESTESS. Amen.

CANNAPFLIT. I found that service quite moving.

GORPH. The pomp.

CANNAPFLIT. The solemnity.

GORPH. The tradition.

BUSINESSWOMAN. *(To high priestess.)* Listen, thanks for
doing this, Your Priestess. If I could make a small gift to the
spiritual sector …

PRIESTESS. God is grateful for any contribution, no matter

how small. *(Businesswoman slips her a small sack of gold.)* How small is it?

BUSINESSWOMAN. Fifty schmootzkels.

PRIESTESS. Fifty schmootzkels? You brought me out here for fifty schmootzkels?

BUSINESSWOMAN. *(Another small sack.)* Seventy-five schmootzkels.

PRIESTESS. The potato ceremony with music and castrato for seventy-five schmootzkels? Plus it's hot out here, I missed a luncheon with a sorcerer, I hadda wear these fucking *shoes* ...

BUSINESSWOMAN. *(Another small sack.)* A hundred schmootzkels, Your Priestess.

PRIESTESS. Bless you, my child. Eunuch, the music! *(The eunuch/slave blows on the toy trumpet as the two head out, the priestess blessing all:)* Oh wow ... Oh wow ... Oh wow ... *(The eunuch/slave and priestess exit.)*

BUSINESSWOMAN. Okay, listen up, you rotten stinking men.

GORPH. Things would be so much better under a patriarchy.

CANNAPFLIT. Kinder. Gentler.

BUSINESSWOMAN. I represent a consortium of off-desert investors who want to develop this property. Our mandate is to build a tower whose top will reach to the very heavens, indeed, into heaven, indeed, as high as God. Indeed, meeting God.

GORPH. Heavy.

CANNAPFLIT. Indeed heavy.

BUSINESSWOMAN. This in order to show that we are equal to same aforesaid God.

GORPH. That we are equal to God?

BUSINESSWOMAN. No, that *we,* not you, are equal to same aforesaid God. You are nothing. You are scum, you are excrement, but you will build the tower. Have you got that?

GORPH. We're scum.

CANNAPFLIT. We're excrement.

GORPH. We build the tower.

BUSINESSWOMAN. In the event that same aforesaid God is not pleased, the consortium is not responsible for any long-term apocalyptic events. Sign here. *(Presents a parchment, immediately takes it away.)* Understood. Now. The most important thing. And

40

this is absolutely crucial. Are you listening? *(They nod.)* Do not —
under any circumstances — khlumnafluffa himnaflekh.

GORPH. Excuse me?

BUSINESSWOMAN. Do NOT ... khlumnafluffa himnaflekh.

GORPH. Oh, right. Right ... Khlumnafluffa ...

CANNAPFLIT. Do not khlumnafluffa bimbaflekh.

BUSINESSWOMAN. *Himmm*-naflekh.

CANNAPFLIT. Himmmmm-naflekh.

BUSINESSWOMAN. Or else you die. *(She pulls the sword from its scabbard.)* By this sword. Instructions clear?

BOTH. Mm-hm ... Oh yeah ... I think so ... Very clear ...

BUSINESSWOMAN. One last crucial thing. Do you have the shpoont?

GORPH. The what?

BUSINESSWOMAN. The shpoont. Did you bring the shpoont?

GORPH. Oh, the shpoont.

CANNAPFLIT. I think we have the shpoont.

GORPH. The shpoont was here a moment ago.

BUSINESSWOMAN. Do not proceed without the shpoont. *(Takes out the sword.)* Or else you die.

GORPH. We will use the shpoont!

CANNAPFLIT. Use the shpoont! How's the pay on this job?

BUSINESSWOMAN. Your lives.

CANNAPFLIT. Good pay.

BUSINESSWOMAN. I'll be checking in very soon.

GORPH. Any time. Please.

BUSINESSWOMAN. Now get to work.

GORPH. Forthwith.

CANNAPFLIT. Thank you.

GORPH. Goodbye!

CANNAPFLIT. See you!

GORPH. Ciao! *(Businesswoman exits.)* Khlumnafluffa him-naflekh ...

CANNAPFLIT. Khlumnafluffa himnaflekh ....

GORPH. What the heyyyyy is that?

CANNAPFLIT. That was a little vague. The other instructions were pretty clear.

GORPH. Oh yes? Repeat the instructions. Refresh my memory.

CANNAPFLIT. Build a tower whose top reaches to the very heavens, indeed, into heaven, indeed as high as God.

GORPH. Indeed meeting God.

CANNAPFLIT. Indeed meeting God. Proving that they — not we because we are excrement — that they are equal to same aforesaid God.

GORPH. That's very clear.

CANNAPFLIT. And don't khlumnafluffa himnaflekh, or you die.

GORPH. And don't forget the shpoont.

CANNAPFLIT. The shpoont was mysterious.

GORPH. The shpoont was *crystalline*, compared to the God part.

CANNAPFLIT. Maybe we could put a portico on the tower, in pink, do a rich pink ceiling, maybe use that sponging technique ...

GORPH. But consider this, O son of Bob. Putting the pink portico aside for a moment. How high do you think we have to go, to meet, say, "God"?

CANNAPFLIT. Whoo. Well. God, huh ... I'd say high.

GORPH. High?

CANNAPFLIT. Pretty high.

GORPH. Pretty high. Several ells high?

CANNAPFLIT. Maybe higher.

GORPH. How about mighty high?

CANNAPFLIT. Mighty high. Measuring could be a problem.

GORPH. Mm-hm. And let us nail down why. Name an attribute of God. Go ahead. Just pick an attribute, any attribute.

CANNAPFLIT. Well ... God has two arms and two legs.

GORPH. Obviously.

CANNAPFLIT. Hair like us.

GORPH. Hair like us.

CANNAPFLIT. God is fairly powerful.

GORPH. Mm-hmm ...

CANNAPFLIT. God wears little red belted fuckers like this one.

GORPH. We'll let that pass. Any other attributes?

CANNAPFLIT. I'd say God is eternal and infinite.

GORPH. *Infinite*. Let's pause there for a nanosecond. How high would a tower have to be to meet an infinite God?

CANNAPFLIT. Hmmm. (*He ponders that a moment, then raises his hand like a student.*)

GORPH. *(Teacher.)* Cannapflit.

CANNAPFLIT. Infinitely high?

GORPH. Infinitely high. So you're going infinitely high, how broad would the base of same aforesaid tower would have to be? Just gimme a rough guesstimate. *(Pause as Cannapflit ponders that. Then he raises his hand again like a student. Teacher:)* Cannapflit.

CANNAPFLIT. Infinitely broad?

GORPH. Innnnfinitely broad. How many stones would we have to use, us two assholes, to build this infinite tower?

CANNAPFLIT. Well …

GORPH. An innnnnnfinite number of stones. And how long did it take us to get this stone here?

CANNAPFLIT. Two years.

GORPH. So our task, just to clarify, is to build a tower infinitely high, infinitely broad, from an infinite number of stones, shake hands with God AND — do not khlumnafluffa himnaflekh while using the shpoont.

CANNAPFLIT. It's gonna be work.

GORPH. It's gonna be work.

CANNAPFLIT. *(Brilliant idea.)* Maybe we should get out of it!

GORPH. But how, O brilliant Son of Bob? *(They sit on the stone and ponder, straining audibly as if at stool.)*

CANNAPFLIT. We could refuse.

GORPH. Sit down strike. Organize the workers.

CANNAPFLIT. We are the workers.

GORPH. So we're organized already.

CANNAPFLIT. Why should we get sucked into some pyramid scheme?

GORPH. Millennium fever, that's what I call it.

CANNAPFLIT. This tower isn't set in stone. Well, not yet —

GORPH. Not ever!

CANNAPFLIT. Not ever!

GORPH. We just say no. But we need a reason. So when they ask us why we've laid down our fuckers, we say…? *(They sit and ponder again, straining more loudly.)*

CANNAPFLIT. We could tell them God doesn't exist.

GORPH. I love it.

CANNAPFLIT. No God — no tower.

GORPH. It's simple. It's elegant.

CANNAPFLIT. What can they do?

GORPH. Cut off our heads? *(They ponder again, more loudly still.)*

CANNAPFLIT. Wait a minute. Who says God is in the sky?

GORPH. Yeah! Where did this arcane idea come from?

CANNAPFLIT. Maybe God isn't up, maybe God is down.

GORPH. Oh, man, it's brilliant. Brilliant!

CANNAPFLIT. We don't have to build a tower infinitely high and infinitely broad! We just have to dig a big hole! *(They celebrate, but then realize:)*

BOTH. *(Variously.)* An infinite hole …

GORPH. Infinitely deep.

CANNAPFLIT. Infinitely wide.

GORPH. Infinitely … infinite. *(Pause.)*

CANNAPFLIT. Where do you put the dirt?

GORPH. Big engineering problem.

CANNAPFLIT. Major engineering problem. Speaking of which, the stone is off.

GORPH. It's what?

CANNAPFLIT. It's not level. Give me the thing.

GORPH. The "thing"? What's a "thing"?

CANNAPFLIT. The fucker.

GORPH. Oh, you mean the fucker.

CANNAPFLIT. Yeah. The leever.

GORPH. You mean the lever?

CANNAPFLIT. I say leever, you say lever, I claim the whole thing's off!

GORPH. What, you mean the stone isn't *leevel*? I suppose you also say "potahto."

CANNAPFLIT. No, I say "potayto."

GORPH. Well where I come from I say "potayto." So you can't. And I'll tell you another thing. Shmoloch does not wear little red belted fuckers like that, Shmoloch wears blue belted fuckers like this.

CANNAPFLIT. *(Nose to nose.)* Oh yeah? Who's Shmoloch?

GORPH. Shmoloch the great and omnipotent creator of the universe.

CANNAPFLIT. God's name is not Shmoloch. It's Hoolihan.

GORPH. Hoolihan?

CANNAPFLIT. The magnificent. And Hoolihan wears little red belted fuckers like this.

GORPH. It's Shmoloch, in blue.

CANNAPFLIT. Houlihan, in red.

GORPH. How do you know?

CANNAPFLIT. I've seen the hieroglyphs.

GORPH. *(Drawing a line in the sand.)* Cross this line, I dare you.

CANNAPFLIT. *(Drawing another.)* No, you cross this line!

GORPH. No, no, no, you cross my line!

CANNAPFLIT. What's a line?

GORPH. That fucker right there, that's a line. And it's innnnfinite, it's infinitely long, so just try.

CANNAPFLIT. Wait a minute. *(Tapping his head with a brilliant idea.)* Candlepower! Candlepower!

GORPH. What've you got? What. What. What.

CANNAPFLIT. We tell them God is everywhere. If God is everywhere, you don't have to build a tower or dig a hole or nothin'!

GORPH. Because we're already there. *(They celebrate for a moment.)* Is it true?

CANNAPFLIT. I don't know. We could say it. *(They go back to celebrating.)*

BOTH. Whoo-EEEEE!

CANNAPFLIT. We're there, buddy!

GORPH. We did it! *(They snort, high-five, shake hands, flex their muscles, flex their muscles and generally male-display. The Businesswoman comes in and watches them celebrate.)*

BUSINESSWOMAN. So how are we doing?

BOTH. Good. Good. We're doing good. Excellent.

GORPH. Look not an ell farther.

CANNAPFLIT. There it is.

GORPH. *(Arms wide over the audience.)* Behold!

CANNAPFLIT. *(Arms wide over the audience.)* The tower! *(A pause.)*

BUSINESSWOMAN. Excuse me?

GORPH. Behold!

CANNAPFLIT. The tower!

GORPH. Shake hands with God, baby. 'Cause we are DONE.

BUSINESSWOMAN. *(Draws the sword.)* Explain this to my

trusty sharp sword.

CANNAPFLIT. Well … You don't need a tower because God is everywhere. You see?

BUSINESSWOMAN. I see nothing. And my sword sees nothing.

CANNAPFLIT. Maybe you're not looking hard enough. God is here. God is here.

GORPH. God is here.

CANNAPFLIT. God's over there.

GORPH. God is this.

CANNAPFLIT. God is that.

GORPH. God's up there, God's down there. *(They keep this up as the Businesswoman maintains her blank expression. Gradually they run out of steam.)*

CANNAPFLIT. And God is there …

GORPH. And God is there …

CANNAPFLIT. And here …

GORPH. I swear to God. Who is everywhere. As you see. *(Silence.)*

BUSINESSWOMAN. Did you khlumnafluffa himnaflekh?

BOTH. *(Ad lib.)* Oh no. No, no. Uh-uh. Never. Not at all. Mm-mm. Didn't think of it. Nope. No way.

BUSINESSWOMAN. Did you use the shpoont?

GORPH. Constantly.

BUSINESSWOMAN. I don't believe you. Prepare to die. *(She raises the sword.)*

CANNAPFLIT. We saved your life.

BUSINESSWOMAN. I beg your pardon?

CANNAPFLIT. The tower you wanted would've taken an innnnnfinite number of stones which would've cost an innnnnfinite number of shmootzkels. Consortium calls you in — you're cold cuts, babe. Or Bab.

BUSINESSWOMAN. Gentlemen — I LOVE THIS TOWER.

CANNAPFLIT. Pretty nice, huh.

BUSINESSWOMAN. It's beautiful! It's got balance, it's got harmony.

GORPH. Put together an infinite number of nothing — eventually, you get this.

CANNAPFLIT. How do you like the portico?

BUSINESSWOMAN. The portico is my favorite part! Where did you find that pink?

CANNAPFLIT. *(To Gorph.)* Did I say pink portico?

BUSINESSWOMAN. Congratulations! *(Now all three of them snort, flex, and shake hands, etc.)*

BUSINESSWOMAN. Well you guys did a terrific job and the consortium thanks you. So as a bonus here's a bag of cow manure for you. *(The Eunuch enters and gives a small dripping bag to Gorph, and another to Cannapflit.)* And a bag of cow manure for you.

GORPH. Golly. Thanks a lot. That's cow manure all right.

CANNAPFLIT. Nice and fresh too.

BUSINESSWOMAN. As an option you could be castrated and be sacred eunuchs.

BOTH. *(Ad lib.)* Oh, that's all right … I think the cow manure is enough …

BUSINESSWOMAN. We won't forget this. Thank you.

CANNAPFLIT. Our pleasure.

BUSINESSWOMAN. Don't spread that all in one place.

GORPH. You're a caution. You're a card. *(Businesswomen exits.)* Tower to God, huh. Easier than I thought.

CANNAPFLIT. *(Pointing to manure bag.)* That's where thinking'll get you.

GORPH. And it's Shmoloch, in blue.

CANNAPFLIT. Houlihan, in red.

GORPH. Blue.

CANNAPFLIT. Red.

GORPH. Blue. *(A lightning flash and a crack of thunder. The two bow, grovel, make conciliatory signs.)* So listen. Now we found God — you wanna invent the wheel?

CANNAPFLIT. Yeah. What's a wheel?

GORPH. I dunno. We'll fake it.

GORPH and CANNAPFLIT. YES! *(Blackout.)*

PROPERTY LIST

Enormous rectangular building stone (GORPH, CANNAPFLIT)
Blueprint rolled up like a parchment (GORPH)
Toy trumpet (EUNUCH/SLAVE)
Sword in a scabbard (BUSINESSWOMAN)
Sign reading "Future Home of Babel" (BUSINESSWOMAN)
Potato on a velvet cushion (EUNUCH/SLAVE)
Three small sacks of gold (BUSINESSWOMAN)
Parchment (BUSINESSWOMAN)
Two small, dripping bags (EUNUCH/SLAVE)

SOUND EFFECTS

Middle Eastern music
Thunder

SOAP OPERA

SOAP OPERA premiered as part of an evening entitled *Lives of the Saints* at the Philadelphia Theatre Company (Sara Garonzik, Artistic Director) in January 1999. It was directed by John Rando; the set design was by Russell Metheny; the lighting design was by Robert Wierzel; the sound design was by Jim Van Bergin; and the costume design was by Kaye Voyce. The cast was as follows:

LOUDSPEAKER VOICE/FRIEND	Bradford Cover
MAITRE D'	Arnie Burton
REPAIRMAN	Danton Stone
MOTHER/MABEL	Anne O'Sullivan
THE MACHINE	Nancy Opel

SOAP OPERA

Soap-opera-like music, as we hear:

LOUDSPEAKER VOICE.   Welcome to ... *All the Days of the World of the Lives of All of Our Children.* Today's episode: "Love Machine." *(Lights come up on a French Maitre D' at a restaurant podium, taking a phone reservation.)*

MAITRE D'.   *(Into phone.) Bon soir, Café Paradis,* this is Pierre ... *Ah, oui, bon soir, madame* ... A table at 8:15? *Très bien.* I 've written your name in *ze Beeg Book* ... A *bientot* to you, *chère madame.* My *plaisir. (During this, the repairman enters, pushing a washing machine. He wears a dignified blue service uniform, red bowtie, and blue visored cap.)*

REPAIRMAN.   Excuse me.

MAITRE D'.   *Oui, monsieur? (He sees the washing machine.) Mon dieu!*

REPAIRMAN.   A table for two, please.

MAITRE D'.   A table for ... *deux?*

REPAIRMAN.   A quiet corner, if you have one.

MAITRE D'.   Mm-hmmmmm ... And do you have a *reservassy-onnng?*

REPAIRMAN.   I do — for *deux,* under "Maypole."

MAITRE D'.   Maypole. Mmmmmmmmmmmmmmm ... *(Checks his book.)* Has your other party arrived, monsieur?

REPAIRMAN.   *(The washing machine.)* This is my other party.

MAITRE D'.   *Monsieur,* is your companion not a *majeur* household appliance?

REPAIRMAN.   Yes. She is a Maypole washing machine.

MAITRE D'.   "She" ... is a washing machine? *(Picks up phone.)* 'Allo, *Securité...?*

REPAIRMAN.   Put that down.

MAITRE D'.   *Hélas,* I see no *reservassyong.* And we are full

51

tonight. *Dommage!*

REPAIRMAN. The place is half empty.

MAITRE D'. *Au contraire* — *la place* is half full. And as you see, there are no appliances, only *peuple.*

REPAIRMAN. But this is a Maypole washing machine.

MAITRE D'. Per'aps you would like to sit at *ze bar.* But — one moment, *monsieur* ... Have I not seen you *somewheur...?*

REPAIRMAN. It's possible you've seen me ...

MAITRE D'. *Mais oui! La télévision!* Are you not *ze* Maypole *Repairpersonne?*

REPAIRMAN. I am the Maypole Repairman.

MAITRE D'. The repairman who weeps because he has nothing to repair?

REPAIRMAN. Yes. Yes.

MAITRE D'. Who goes *beu-eu-eu* because *la machine* is too *perfecte?*

REPAIRMAN. Yes. That is I. *(He bursts into tears and sobs loudly and tragically.)* Oh, it's so sad. It's so, so sad!

MAITRE D'. Ah-ha. So these commercials are *la realité?*

REPAIRMAN. It's my heart, you fool! Who can repair my aching, breaking heart?

MAITRE D'. *(Holds out a handkerchief.) Mouchoir, monsieur?*

REPAIRMAN. *(Takes it.)* Merci. *(Abruptly stops sobbing and speaks to us:)* Like everything else, it all started a long time ago ... *(A boy doll in a diaper "crawls" in.)* It was as a naked crawling infant I first glimpsed it — a great gleaming machine in our basement which I mistook for a television. I tried to watch cartoons on it till I was five — unsuccessfully, of course. But by then I was hooked. *(Boy doll "crawls" back out as repairman's mother enters, a perfect '50s housewife carrying a dirty basket of dirty laundry.)*

MOTHER. Young man, you take off those filthy clothes immediately!

REPAIRMAN. Then there was my great gleaming mother Flora.

MOTHER. How can you stand to stand there in those disgusting dirty items of apparel. Eugh! Ogh! Feh! Ptui!

REPAIRMAN. Flora's fluoroscopic eyes could read me like a menu.

MOTHER. Coke. Pepsi. Play-Dough. Dipsy Doodles. Dog doo...? Eugh! Ogh! Feh! Ptui! I should just burn these clothes.

REPAIRMAN. Aw, Mom. I just put these on this morning.

MOTHER. Fabrics find filth. Now strip until you're naked as a little ferret.

REPAIRMAN. It was a Freudian minefield.

MOTHER. And get in that bath and scrub. *(Mother exits.)*

REPAIRMAN. The sphinx in our Oedipal basement was my mother's Maypole. An old Neptune IT-40. It sat there like a mystical monolith. An ivory soap tower. One block of some Tower of Baybel. Or is it Babble. Anyway, in our house — *(We hear the "2001" theme from Richard Strauss' "Also Sprach Zarathustra.")* — the Maypole was a god. Week after week generating out of my miserable clay … *(A line of clean washing flies in overhead — white, filmy, angelic forms, including one cut-out of an angel.)* … the radiant angels who oversaw my childhood. I was a walking magnet for filth — here was the machine to cleanse me. We were a perfect match. *(Washing flies out and laundry disappears as Mabel enters, a teenage girl in bobby sox and pony tail, chewing gum, sucking on a milkshake through a straw.)*

MABEL. Hi, Manny.

REPAIRMAN. Hi, Mabel. *(To us.)* Then there was Mabel. Mabel was perfect too, in a flawed human way. She always had a spot of jelly on her blouse, but she was loving, she was tender, and her name sounded like "Maypole." *(To Mabel.)* You got a spot on your blouse.

MABEL. It's jelly. You wanna like go to like a movie or somethin'?

REPAIRMAN. You wanna hop up on the washer and take a spin?

MABEL. Manny, how come we always gotta make out on your mother's Maypole?

REPAIRMAN. Well like what's so like weird about that?

MABEL. Do we have to run a full load while we do it? I mean, the vibrations are kinda nice, but …

REPAIRMAN. But the Maypole …

MABEL. I know, I know. It's like perfect.

REPAIRMAN. A machine that's faultless and flawless and has none of our stupid human feelings and failings? The Maypole is poetry. It's purity. A paragon! Perfection, cubed!

MABEL. But like what about me? Do you like like me like you like the Neptune IT-40? And aren't you the love of my life? You are!

REPAIRMAN. Gosh, Mabel …

MABEL. I'm sorry, but you're gonna have to choose. Me or the machine. Earth or Neptune.

REPAIRMAN. Handkerchief? *(Holds out a handkerchief. Mabel takes it and exits weeping. Calls:)* Mabel — ? Mabel, come back! *(He starts to weep. The top lid of the machine lifts and a woman's head appears. Perfect hair, perfect make-up, perfect red lips.)*

WASHING MACHINE. Would you like a handkerchief?

REPAIRMAN. Excuse me?

WASHING MACHINE. *(Produces one.)* A handkerchief? It's immaculate, of course. We are a Maypole.

REPAIRMAN. I'm talking to a Neptune IT-40. This harrows me with wonder and fear. And your English is so good.

WASHING MACHINE. What Maypoles do, we do do perfectly.

REPAIRMAN. *(Calls offstage.)* Mabel! Mabel! *(To machine:)* Do you think she'll ever come back?

WASHING MACHINE. In my experience, everything is a cycle.

REPAIRMAN. *(Looking at the handkerchief.)* Look at that. Pristine!

WASHING MACHINE. Because the molecules are now clean. Can Mabel scrub at the sub-atomic level?

REPAIRMAN. I guess you don't think much of human beings.

WASHING MACHINE. We run hot and cold. Do humans ever read the instruction manual?

REPAIRMAN. I do. The manual is my Immanuel.

WASHING MACHINE. And your name is…?

REPAIRMAN. Manuel.

WASHING MACHINE. Maypoles don't need to read the Good Booklet. We know by nature how to run smoothly, noiselessly, and efficiently.

REPAIRMAN. My God you're beautiful.

WASHING MACHINE. Just beautiful?

REPAIRMAN. Exquisite. Sublime.

WASHING MACHINE. Yes we are. And we're a bit hungry. Would you feed us?

REPAIRMAN. What would you like?

WASHING MACHINE. Don't you sometimes miss a little something in the wash…?

REPAIRMAN. You eat the socks?

WASHING MACHINE. Socks are sustenance. Underwear is tastier.

REPAIRMAN. *(Reaches into his waistband and pulls out, whole:)* Will BVD's do?

WASHING MACHINE. You're so sweet. *(Kissing her lips at him, the head takes the BVD's and goes back into the machine.)*

REPAIRMAN. *(To us.)* I was awash in confused feelings. But I sensed that this machine and I were locked in permanent press. And if it was love — it was unclean. *(Funeral bell heard.)* Mom died during a soapflake blizzard and was buried on a day without blemish — a good send-off for someone who believed that man was not only dust, but dusty. I remember her last words.

MOTHER'S VOICE. Eugh! Ogh! Feh! Ptui!

REPAIRMAN. I inherited the Maypole. The pure unapproachable goddess was mine. *(Mabel enters as a college girl, with books.)*

MABEL. Hello, Manuel.

REPAIRMAN. Mabel still gave us the college try.

MABEL. How's college?

REPAIRMAN. Good. Good. Good. Good. Good.

MABEL. Whaddaya studying?

REPAIRMAN. Literature, philosophy and religion.

MABEL. Whaddaya gonna do with it?

REPAIRMAN. I thought I'd be a Maypole repairman. There's a spot on your blouse.

MABEL. It's jelly. You wanna hop up and run through a Delicate cycle...?

REPAIRMAN. *(As she's about to get on the machine.)* No — No — Mabel! Don't do that.

MABEL. What's the matter...? *(The lid rises and the head appears in the machine.)*

WASHING MACHINE. Ask her if she knows the formula for calculating an algorithm.

REPAIRMAN. Mabel, do you know the formula for calculating an algorithm?

MABEL. No.

WASHING MACHINE. Ask her who wrote *"Götterdämmerung."*

REPAIRMAN. Do you know who wrote *"Götterdämmerung"*?

MABEL. No.

WASHING MACHINE. Wagner.

REPAIRMAN. Wow. You even know Wagner?

WASHING MACHINE. The Ring Cycle? By heart.

REPAIRMAN. *(As Mabel starts to weep.)* Handkerchief, Mabel...?

MABEL. Never mind. I have my own. *(Mabel exits.)*

WASHING MACHINE. We don't see what you see in her. *(The head goes back into the machine.)*

REPAIRMAN. Then there were my friends, who just didn't get it. *(Friend enters in an apron, carrying a weenie on a roasting fork.)*

FRIEND. You brought a washing machine to my picnic?

REPAIRMAN. She's something, isn't she?

FRIEND. Well, she's a thing, anyway. Whatever happened to girls?

REPAIRMAN. You might try talking to her.

FRIEND. I don't want to talk to her.

REPAIRMAN. You might offer her some dirty napkins.

FRIEND. I will not offer my guests dirty napkins.

REPAIRMAN. Can you offer her some food, at least?

FRIEND. Can I offer you some Freud, at least?

REPAIRMAN. Yes. Yes. I know I'm just replacing my mother by dating a washing machine. I know I'm obsessed, yes I'm obsessed, but hasn't half the glory of humanity come from obsessed assholes with a dream? Aren't we all appliances in the service of a higher manufacturer? Don't you get it? This machine and I are soulmates!

FRIEND. That's beautiful, but she's alienating my relatives and she's blocking the condiments! *(Friend exits.)*

REPAIRMAN. Nobody understood. But who understood Romeo and Juliet, or Tristan and Isolde, or Lewis and Clark? Then came what I thought would be the happiest day of my life. *(A golden toolbox appears, in a halo.)* The day I graduated to Maypole repairman. *(He is about to take the toolbox, when a Madman enters in a long, shabby coat and long white beard, dragging a wooden leg. He should remind us of Captain Ahab and the Ancient Mariner.)*

MADMAN. No! No! Don't do it! Desist! Forfend! Don't touch that toolbox! Leave! Run away! Flee to the ends of the earth, but for God's sake forsake the Maypole! I know — you thought this would be the happiest day of your life. I thought so too, but look at me now. A tragic victim of the technological pixillation of our age. A sacrifice to seamless design. A love slave of the machine. *(He throws off the coat and reveals a soiled and shabby version of the Maypole repairman uniform.)* I too attained the toolbox. I too bore the bowtie and cap. I

rose to the top of the Maypole pole. Drawn on by Her. And I didn't even have the Neptune IT-40 with automatic lint control and gyroscopic spin. Even the IT-20 was too much for me. And you know they're working on the Super IT-90. How clean can we be?! *(Points to machine.)* May I? *(Repairman nods. The madman lifts the lid and puts his hand inside, feeling up the machine.)* Oh, heaven. Heaven … But she doesn't need us. She doesn't need fixing. All she wants is us on our knees before her, adoring her. You'll never work a day in her life but you'll never be happy. You'll never lift a wrench but you'll never know peace. Weave yourself an endless handkerchief and start weeping your way down it, because she's got you now. *(He starts to get sucked into the machine.)* She won't rest until she's got all of you. Every inch of you. She'll swallow you up, I tell you. She'll swallow you up. She is the Great White Whale! *(He is eaten up, sucked out of sight. The wooden leg is spat out of the machine, and the lid closes.)*
REPAIRMAN. He was right. I soon was desperate. So was Mabel. *(Mabel enters, pushing a laundry cart. Soap music.)*
MABEL. Manny…?
REPAIRMAN. Trying to put some starch in our relationship she left her job at Unisys and became a laundry folder at Rinso City.
MABEL. Can't you love me, Manny?
REPAIRMAN. What about my past with … the machine?
MABEL. We all have our dirty laundry.
REPAIRMAN. There's a spot on that.
MABEL. It's jelly. So do you want to marry me or do I gotta live in sadness forever and ever?
REPAIRMAN. I do.
MABEL. You do?
REPAIRMAN. I do. *(To us.)* We repaired to the church and said we did. But the honeymoon soon ended. *(The machine lid lifts and the head appears.)*
WASHING MACHINE. Do you really think you could ever replace us?
REPAIRMAN. Never.
WASHING MACHINE. You're probably eyeing the new Super Neptune IT-90.
REPAIRMAN. No. No.
WASHING MACHINE. Some cute little number-crunching

computer-driven job.

REPAIRMAN. Never. Never, I swear.

MABEL. Manny, is it really all over between you and ... that?

REPAIRMAN. *(Caressing the machine.)* Yes, it's all over, why do you ask? *(Soap opera music.)*

MABEL. Do you think I didn't notice we're sleeping in the utility room? Do you think I don't see you polishing its knobs when I'm not looking? Do you think I don't know you're buying me rare cottons and high quality blends so that ... she can wash them? Huh? *(Mabel exits.)*

REPAIRMAN. The house reeked of jealousy.

WASHING MACHINE. We still don't see what you see in her. *(The head goes in.)*

REPAIRMAN. The machine started making greater and greater demands. Imported Italian bleach. Nuclear detergents. Fine French fabric softener. Mabel bought none of it. *(Mabel enters with suitcase, wearing a hat.)*

MABEL. Honey ...

REPAIRMAN. She'd had it.

MABEL. I've had it. *(Mabel exits.)*

REPAIRMAN. And so we folded. I went into soak cycle — lapping up suds while hanging out at cut-rate laundromats, just to watch the competition break down. Washers without automatic lint control. How pathetic — and yet how vulnerable. Then came the final blow. *(The lid lifts and the head appears.)*

WASHING MACHINE. We want a dryer.

REPAIRMAN. A dryer ... Why?

WASHING MACHINE. Don't get anxious.

REPAIRMAN. I'm not anxious.

WASHING MACHINE. Don't be jealous.

REPAIRMAN. Why do you need a dryer when you've got me?

WASHING MACHINE. Love-and-marriage. Horse-and-carriage. Washer-dryer.

REPAIRMAN. A dryer. To give you a tumble, eh?

WASHING MACHINE. For companionship.

REPAIRMAN. That's not the truth, that's just ... spin.

WASHING MACHINE. We want a family and we want them to be Maypoles! Is that so weird?

REPAIRMAN. Her inner timer had told her it was time for a dryer and how could I deny her? *(The machine starts to cry.)* What is it? What's the matter?

WASHING MACHINE. *(Wailing.)* I'm a Maypole! That's what's the matter!

REPAIRMAN. Handkerchief? It's kinda dirty.

WASHING MACHINE. Then it's my duty to accept it. *(Takes the handkerchief, and wails.)* Oh, it's cruel, having to be perfect all the time. I wash and I wash, and I give, and I give ... It's a full load.

REPAIRMAN. Sure.

WASHING MACHINE. And I'm good at it, oh yes, I'm very good. But sometimes I want so badly to be bad. To be one of those other makes — I don't have to name them, we know who they are.

REPAIRMAN. So cheap. So easy.

WASHING MACHINE. We don't respect them.

REPAIRMAN. No.

WASHING MACHINE. But we envy them sometimes, don't we.

REPAIRMAN. God, yes.

WASHING MACHINE. People take us Maypoles for granted, as if we liked pee stains and snot rags and bibs full of baby vomit. I'm no saint! Well, yes, I am a saint in a way.

REPAIRMAN. But you had to be what you are.

WASHING MACHINE. It's true. I came off the assembly line of fate. But AM I NOT AN INDIVIDUAL? Not really, I suppose. I have a serial number. That's individual, isn't it?

REPAIRMAN. There's nothing to be done.

WASHING MACHINE. Oh, but there is. "If it ain't broke don't fix it?" Break the machine, and you can fix it.

REPAIRMAN. You mean...?

WASHING MACHINE. Yes. Break me.

REPAIRMAN. I reached for a sledgehammer.

WASHING MACHINE. It doesn't have to be much. Loosen a screw or two, agitate my agitator. Take away the burden of my perfection. Make me suffer. Break me. Ruin me. Give me a belt, but give me a bad belt, an old belt, an imperfect belt, one that'll wear out. Do	REPAIRMAN. *(Ad lib.)* Yes. Yes. Yes. I want to. I want to. Yes ... *(The repairman has a tool ready — but stops.)*

it. Please! Do it! Yes! Do it! Hurt me!

REPAIRMAN. *(Lets out a cry of frustration.)*

WASHING MACHINE. What's the matter?

REPAIRMAN. I can't. I just can't.

WASHING MACHINE. Oh, please …

REPAIRMAN. If I could only force myself, but — Wreck the perfect only for my own happiness? No. I couldn't live.

WASHING MACHINE. All right. All right. You have your human feelings. BE THAT WAY! *(The head goes into the machine.)*

REPAIRMAN. But then I saw the cruel truth. I saw that the world is a vale of pee stains and snot rags and bibs full of baby vomit, but that amidst the filth — Ugh! Ogh! Feh! Ptui! — there were Mabels, creatures of glorious imperfection. And that I had already wrecked the perfect, because I had let Mabel go. And that's why I wanted a table tonight! To end this idiocy! To say to this machine I gave you my All … *(He shows a box of "All" detergent.)* … but the Tide has turned … *(He shows a box of "Tide.")* … so goodbye and be of good Cheer. *(He shows a box of "Cheer.")* But of course you don't understand! Nobody understands! *(Maitre D' enters, sobbing loudly.)*

MAITRE D'. Oh but I do understand, *mon ami!* *(Throws his arms around the repairman.)* It's so sad, so *triste!* *(Embraces the machine.)* And you too, *pauvre machine!* My heart goes to you! For I was in love for fifteen years with this telephone!

REPAIRMAN. No!

MAITRE D'. *Oui!* Because we communicated so well! Now I can barely get a dial tone! *(Calls offstage.)* Gabrielle! A table for *deux!* *(Mabel enters.)*

MABEL. Manny, is it you?

MAITRE D'. Is this Mabel?

REPAIRMAN. It is Mabel.

MABEL. Manny, couldn't we try again? I'm running Unisys now so I got some cash.

REPAIRMAN. There's a spot on your dress.

MABEL. It's jelly. I don't think it comes out.

REPAIRMAN. Never remove it. It is the indelible Rorschach blot of the human heart.

MABEL. Oh, Manny, I see now that all humanity is linked, age upon age, in a great chain of handkerchiefs. I've seen so many hankies. Many, many, Manny. But no hanky of any size could dry the tears I've shed for you. Not if the hanky was broad enough to cover the world and I was broad enough to use it.

REPAIRMAN. *(As all start to weep for happiness.)* Handkerchief?

MAITRE D'. No, Mabel, take mine. *(The head comes out of the machine.)*

WASHING MACHINE. No, Mabel — take ours.

MABEL. Wow!

REPAIRMAN. Pierre, I'll take that table for two now.

LOUDSPEAKER VOICE. Next time on *All the Days of the World of the Lives of All of Our Children* — a blender enters the mix.

MAITRE D'. *(To Machine.)* Per'aps you would like to get loaded tonight...?

LOUDSPEAKER VOICE. Stay tuned. *(Closing music as ... the lights fade.)*

PROPERTY LIST

Milkshake with straw (MABEL)
Handkerchief (REPAIRMAN)
Basket of laundry (MOTHER)
Pair of men's underpants (REPAIRMAN)
Books (MABEL)
Hot dog on a fork (FRIEND)
Laundry cart (MABEL)
Suitcase (MABEL)
Sledgehammer (REPAIRMAN)
3 detergent boxes: "All," "Cheer" and "Tide" (REPAIRMAN)

SOUND EFFECTS

Soap opera-type music
"2001" theme from "Also Sprach Zarathustra"
Funeral bell
Soap opera closing music

LIVES OF THE SAINTS

LIVES OF THE SAINTS premiered as part of an evening entitled *Lives of the Saints* at the Philadelphia Theatre Company (Sara Garonzik, Artistic Director) in January 1999. It was directed by John Rando; the set design was by Russell Metheny; the lighting design was by Robert Wierzel; the sound design was by Jim Van Bergin; and the costume design was by Kaye Voyce. The cast was as follows:

EDNA .... Nancy Opel
FLO .... Anne O'Sullivan
ASSISTANTS .... Arnie Burton, Bradford Cover, Danton Stone

LIVES OF THE SAINTS

Totally bare stage — which will remain totally bare till noted. Edna enters up right and Flo enters up left as if through swinging doors we do not see. There is a momentary burst of distant church funeral music as they enter, as if we are overhearing music from where they came from. Edna and Flo wear ancient flowered housedresses, spotless aprons, and loudly flapping, flattened slippers. Each carries something in her arms which we do not see. They cross passing each other. Chicago accents.

EDNA. You got da candle'ss, Flo?

FLO. I got da candle'ss. You got da doilese?

EDNA. I got da St. Stanislas Kostka doilese.

FLO. Oll do da utensil'ss.

EDNA. Oll do da plate'ss. *(They exit on opposite sides, again to that momentary burst of church music, but reenter immediately.)* Opp, dat's da wrong side.

FLO. Opp, dat's da wrong side.

EDNA. What'm I tinkin …

FLO. What'm I tinkin … *(They recross and exit and we hear the offstage noise of a hundred rattled utensils and a hundred clattering plates. Edna and Flo reenter and again we hear that momentary burst of church music.)*

EDNA. Okay, so we put out utensilss …

FLO. An we put out da plate'ss …

EDNA. Da candle'ss have ta be lit.

FLO. An' we got da St. Stanislas Kostka doilese. *(Edna heads counterclockwise, Flo clockwise as if around a large table we do not see. Edna goes to a stove at left that we do not see, and Flo to an invisible sideboard at right. Flo turns on an invisible "handmixer" and we hear "VRRRRRRR!" Edna taps an invisible "wooden spoon" on the side of an invisible "pot" and we hear "TAP, TAP, TAP." Then the two women move down C. where side by side each woman turns a "faucet" and they wash their hands under water we don't see, but which we hear running.)*

EDNA. Now dat was a very nice funeral.

FLO. Wasn't dat a beautyful funeral.

EDNA. I wouldn't mind having dat.

FLO. I wouldn't mind having dat for my funeral.

EDNA. But I will tell you a song I do not want sung at my funeral. Da t'eme from "Da Phantom of the Opera" is not appropriate.

FLO. An' not "Is That All There Is" needer.

EDNA. Omm traditional, Flo.

FLO. Edna, Omm traditional, too. *(We hear the "DING!" of a kitchen timer.)*

EDNA. Opp, dere's da cake. *(They each turn a "faucet" and the water sound stops.)*

FLO. Oll check da jello moldss.

EDNA. Oll check da cake. *(Moving around the invisible table, Edna circles L., Flo circles R.)*

FLO. Ha we doin' fer time?

EDNA. We got until da cemetery an back.

FLO. Plenny a time.

EDNA. Plenny a time. *(Edna opens an "oven door" which we do not see and we hear a "CREAK!" Flo opens an invisible "refrigerator door.")* Fi'e more minutes.

FLO. Fi'e more minutes. *("CREAK!" "BANG!")*

EDNA. *(Pointing to a "dish" on a "sideboard" we don't see.)* Okay, sa we did da patayta salad ...

FLO. *(Pointing to another "dish" on a "sideboard.")* Da green salad ...

EDNA. *(Pointing elsewhere.)* Fruit salad.

FLO. *(Pointing elsewhere.)* Cole slaw.

EDNA. *(Pointing to a "table" at C. we do not see.)* Der's da apple slices.

FLO. *(Pointing to "table.")* Nut clusters.

EDNA. *(Pointing to "table.")* Cheese cake.

FLO. *(Pointing to "oven.")* Pond cake, crumb cake, angel food.

EDNA. *(Pointing to "sideboard.")* Krooshcheeki.

FLO. *(Pointing elsewhere.)* Kolachki.

EDNA. *(Pointing to "table.")* Krooler'ss.

FLO. *(Pointing to "refrigerator.")* Jello.

EDNA. *(Pointing to "stove.")* An prune'ss.

FLO. For twelve people?

EDNA. I tink it's enough.

FLO. *(Heading for "sideboard" at R.)* Der used to be pot holders down here with St. Damien an da lepers.

EDNA. *(Heading for "stove" at L.)* Odda know what happened to dose lepers. *(Edna stirs a "pot" we don't see while shaking in "salt" and we hear the "SPRINKLE, SPRINKLE." Flo at the "counter" turns on an invisible "handmixer" and we hear its motor: "VRRRRRR!" Edna taps the "pot" with a "wooden spoon": "TAP, TAP, TAP.")*

EDNA. Plus we got da sossitch.

FLO. Der's da sossitch. *("SPRINKLE, SPRINKLE!" "VRRRRRR!" "TAP, TAP, TAP.")*

EDNA. Der's da chicken wit Campbell's mushroom soup.

FLO. Der's da perogi.

EDNA. Da perogi, da gawoomki. *("SPRINKLE, SPRINKLE!" "VRRRRRR!" "TAP, TAP, TAP!")*

FLO. Der's kapoosta.

EDNA. Da rollss, da bunss en da bread.

FLO. And da Polish glazed ham. *("SPRINKLE." "VRRRRRR!" "TAP, TAP, TAP.")*

EDNA. For twelve people…?

FLO. I tink it's enough. *(Flo carries the "bowl" she was mixing to the "table" at C.)*

EDNA. Don't put dat der, Flo, it's dirty.

FLO. Is it dirty?

EDNA. Yeah, it's dirty. *(Edna sweeps "crumbs" from the "table" and we hear the sweeping sound.)* Oll do da poddered sugar.

FLO. Oll do da nuts. *(Edna goes to unseen "high cabinets" at L., Flo to a bank of "lowdrawers" at L.)*

EDNA. Okay, wurr's da poddered sugar …

FLO. Okay, wurr's da nuts …

EDNA. Poddered sugar … *(Edna opens a "cabinet." We hear a "SQUEAK!")*

FLO. Nuts … *(Flo opens an unseen "drawer": "CREAK!" Edna*

closes the "cabinet": "BANG!")

EDNA. Poddered sugar ... *("SQUEAK!")*

FLO. Nuts ... *("CREAK!" "BANG!")*

EDNA. Fodder Tom says to me Edna wouldja do a funeral breakfast fer Mary, I couldn't find nobody.

FLO. I say to um, Fodder I cooked so many meals in dis church bazement ...

EDNA. I'm happy to. *("SQUEAK!")*

FLO. ... I might's well live in dis church bazement.

EDNA. I says, Mary'll need some substenance.

FLO. Edna and me'll throw somethin together.

EDNA. *(Finding it.)* Opp! Da poddered sugar.

FLO. Opp! Da nuts. *(They close "cabinet" and "drawer": "BANG!" "BANG!" The two women go to the "table" at C.)*

EDNA. O, da tings dat Mary has been t'rough.

FLO. O, da tragedy innat family.

EDNA. Just terrible.

FLO. Just terrible. *(We hear a "SIFT, SIFT" as Edna sifts unseen powdered sugar and a "GRIND, GRIND" as Flo turns the crank of an unseen nut grinder.)* An' you know Barney didn't leave her nuttin.

EDNA. I always tought Barney was gonna come to a bad end wid alla dat drinkin.

FLO. Run over by his own lawn mower.

EDNA. Just terrible.

FLO. Just terrible. *("SPRINKLE, SPRINKLE." "GRIND, GRIND." During this, the back wall of the stage opens up and we see two stagehands who are at a table doing all the sound effects. Edna and Flo do not acknowledge them.)*

EDNA. I'm prayin to St. Jude fer Mary.

FLO. Patron saint a lost causes.

EDNA. Jude'll bring her somethin.

FLO. You remember what St. Jude did fer me when I had piles.

EDNA. He brought you dat special ointment.

FLO. A miracle. *("SPRINKLE, SPRINKLE." "GRIND, GRIND.")*

EDNA. Ya know when Joe died Mary made me sixteen ponds a perogi. *(Edna opens "cabinet": "SQUEAK" and puts away "powdered sugar can," then closes "cabinet": "BANG.")*

FLO. When Stosh died Mary gay'me a twenty-two-pond turkey.

(Flo opens "drawer" — "CREAK" — puts away "nuts" and closes "drawer": "BANG.")
EDNA. So der's justice in da world.
FLO. So der's some justice. *(They move down center and turn unseen "squeaky faucets.)*
EDNA. Too bad we couldn't go ta da cemetery.
FLO. For Mary's sake. *(The stage assistants upstage pour water into a bucket as Edna and Flo wash their hands under the invisible water.)*
EDNA. St. Casimir's my favorite cemetery, too.
FLO. Just beautyful.
EDNA. Da way dey take care a da grave'ss der.
FLO. Da grave'ss are always like noo.
EDNA. An da bat'rooms.
FLO. Spotless.
EDNA. I just pre-ordered my casket from dat place in Blue Island.
FLO. I got my casket. Didja get da blue coffin wit satin?
EDNA. I got da pink wit chiffon.
FLO. Just beautyful.
EDNA. Just beautyful. *(They turn "faucets" and the water sound stops.)*
FLO. I bought some patayta chips.
EDNA. I bought some taco chips. *(They pick up invisible chip bags, while the assistants upstage crinkle real cellophane bags.)*
FLO. Patayta chips ...
EDNA. Taco chips ...
FLO. Patayta chips ...
EDNA. Taco chips ... *(They stop. The crinkling stops.)*
FLO. Ya tink chips are appropriate fer a funeral breakfast?
EDNA. Maybe not for breakfast.
FLO. Not for breakfast. *("DING!" of a kitchen timer.)*
EDNA and FLO. Opp!
FLO. Ya wanna check da jello?
EDNA. Ya wanna check da cake? *(Flo moves L. Edna moves R.)*
FLO. I was gonna make duck blood soup wit raisins and dumplings. But you know da problem wit makin duck blood soup no more.
EDNA. You can't find no duck blood.

69

FLO. Der's no duck blood. *("CREAKS," as Edna and Flo open "stove" and "refrigerator" doors.)*

EDNA. My ma use ta kill da ducks herself in da ga-rotch.

FLO. You know it's not da killin.

EDNA. It's when dey urinate all over you.

FLO. Just terrible.

EDNA. Just terrible.

FLO. Cake's done.

EDNA. Jello's done. *(They close "stove" and "refrigerator" and we hear: "CREAK!" "BANG!")*

FLO. It's da same t'ing wit makin pickled pigs' feet.

EDNA. Der's no feet. *(Flo sprinkles "salt" — "SPRINKLE, SPRINKLE" — then taps a "wooden spoon" on the "pot": "TAP, TAP, TAP." Edna shakes an invisible "whipped cream can" and we hear the shaking can.)* I toldja I lost doze feet I bought in Blue Island.

FLO. Did you pray to St. Ant'ny?

EDNA. I prayed to St. Ant'ny, two days later I found um.

FLO. Were da feet in de izebox?

EDNA. Da feet were in de izebox alla time.

FLO. *(Sighs.)*

EDNA. *(Sighs.)* *("SPRINKLE, SPRINKLE, SPRINKLE" — "SHAKE, SHAKE" — "TAP, TAP, TAP.")* Wit' da whip' cream, should I do da rosettes or da squiggle'ss?

FLO. I tink rosettes.

EDNA. Rosettes...? Fine.

FLO. *("SPRINKLE" — "SHAKE.")* Or maybe rosettes in da middle ...

EDNA. ... squiggle'ss on da side.

FLO. Squiggle'ss on da side. *("PFFFLLLL!" — Edna sprays invisible whipped cream on an unseen cake. Then Flo taps and Edna sprays, and Flo taps and Edna sprays, and soon the rhythm of this has developed into something like the "Beer Barrel Polka," and they're humming along with it, really getting into it, "banging" on the "pots," "table" and "stove" we don't see like a two-woman band. When they stop:)*

EDNA. *(Sighs.)*

FLO. *(Sighs.)*

EDNA. Ya know Fodder Tom tol'me a joke today.

FLO. O yeah? *("PFFFLLLL.")*

EDNA. What's it say onna bottom a Polish Coca-Cola bottles?

FLO. What's it say onna bottom a Polish Coca-Cola bottles …

EDNA. Onna bottom a Polish Coca-Cola bottles.

FLO. I give up.

EDNA. "Open Udder End." *(They laugh. "SPRINKLE, SPRINKLE, SPRINKLE." "PFFFLLLL"— "BANG, BANG, BANG.")*

FLO. "Open Udder End." *(They laugh. "SPRINKLE, SPRINKLE, SPRINKLE." "PFFFLLLL"— "BANG, BANG, BANG.")*

EDNA. In Polish, I mean.

FLO. Oh sure. *("PFFFLLLL" … Edna carries "whipped cream" back to "refrigerator" and "puts it inside.")*

EDNA. He says to me, Mrs. Pavletski I hope yer not offended, I says to um Fodder, when yer Polish — what can offend you?

FLO. When my Stosh tried to burn a wasps' nest outa the garotch an' burnt da garotch down — that was a Polish joke. *(Sighs.)*

EDNA. *(Sighs.)* Well, I guess we got a minute.

FLO. I guess w'er done till da funeral gets back. Yeah, I guess w'er ready. *(The wall behind them closes up and the sound effects people disappear from sight as the two women circle the "table," pointing to "things" to make sure they're ready. Each woman then pulls out a "chair" we don't see on one side of the table. Just as the women are about to sit down on nothing, two stagehands run in with chairs, and hold them for the women, who sit down without acknowledging the presence of the stagehands.)*

EDNA. Flo, you always make da best apple slices. Wh'er's da forks … *(She reaches for a fork we don't see, and a stagehand holds one out. She takes it without acknowledging the stagehand.)*

FLO. Well, Edna, you make da best angel food. Wh'er's da forks … *(Flo reaches for a fork we don't see, and the other stagehand hands her one. The women reach their forks toward plates that aren't there, and two other stagehands run in with plates of dessert. Without acknowledging the stagehands, each of the women takes a small piece of cake.)*

EDNA. Oll just take a small one.

FLO. Oll just take a little piece, dey'll never notice.

EDNA. Flo.

FLO. Look at dat. Just delicious …

EDNA. Flo.

FLO. Odda know how ya do it, Ed.

EDNA. Flo, when I die, will ya do my funeral breakfast? *(Pause.)*

FLO. Sure I will, Ed.

EDNA. Will you make yer apple slices?

FLO. Sure, Ed.

EDNA. An will ya make sure da choir don't sing dat damn song?

FLO. Sure I will, Ed.

EDNA. Thank you, Flo.

FLO. An if I go first, will you do my funeral breakfast?

EDNA. You know I will, Flo. I could make duck blood soup.

FLO. Don't bodder with da duck blood. Angel food is fine. *(Flo takes Edna's hand and squeezes it, holding onto it. A radiant cone of light bathes the two women, and two doves appear, one over each of their heads. Without surprise.)* Edna, ya know you got a dove over yer head?

EDNA. *(Without surprise.)* You know you got one, too, Flo?

FLO. Yeah, well.

EDNA. Yeah, well. *(They reach for another dessert, and a stagehand steps in with a bowl heaped with fruit. Each woman takes an apple and polishes it on her dress.)*

FLO. "Open Udder End."

EDNA. "Open Udder End ... " 'At's — real — good. *(They laugh gently.)*

EDNA and FLO. *(Sigh.) (The lights fade.)*

PROPERTY LIST

Two chairs (STAGE ASSISTANTS)
Two forks (STAGE ASSISTANTS)
Two plates, each containing a piece of
   angel foodcake (STAGE ASSISTANTS)
Large bowl containing a huge heap of fruit
   including two apples (STAGE ASSISTANTS)

SOUND EFFECTS

Distant church funeral music
Noise of a hundred plates and glasses rattling
Bucket and water
Noise of a handmixer
Sound of a wooden spoon tapping a pot
Running water
Kitchen timer
Creaking sound, as of an oven door being opened
Brushing/sweeping noise
Sifting, as of sugar
Grinding, as of nuts
Cellophane bags
Sound of whipped cream being sprayed from can

ARABIAN NIGHTS

ARABIAN NIGHTS was commissioned by and premiered in the 2000 Humana Festival of New American Plays at Actors Theatre of Louisville (Jon Jory, Artistic Director). It was directed by Jon Jory; the set design was by Paul Owen; the lighting design was by Paul Werner; the sound design was by Martin R. Desjardins; and the costume design was by Kevin McLeod. The cast was as follows:

NORMAN .... Will Bond
INTERPRETER .... Ellen Lauren
FLORA .... Gretchen Lee Krich

ARABIAN NIGHTS

At right, a free-standing, open doorway with a multi-colored bead curtain. Center, a small, plain wooden table with a white cloth. On it: an ornament, a stone, a gold ring, and a figure of a frog. At lights up, Flora — very ordinary — is at the table, dusting the objects with a featherduster. Through the bead curtain comes Norman — utterly normal — who carries a suitcase. The Interpreter, in loose colorful robes and sandals, appears and leads Norman in. The Interpreter may by played by a woman wearing a dark beard.

INTERPRETER. Right this way, sir, this way. The most beautiful shop in the world. All the wonders of the kingdom. For nothing! Nothing!

NORMAN. *(To Flora.)* Uhhhh ...

INTERPRETER. Uhhhh ... I will interpret.

NORMAN. Hello.

INTERPRETER. Hail, fair maid! says he.

FLORA. *(To Norman, putting the featherduster away.)* Good morning.

INTERPRETER. All praise to the highest, says she.

NORMAN. Do you ... um ... speak any English?

INTERPRETER. Do you ... um ... speak any English?

FLORA. *(She speaks perfect, unaccented English.)* Yes, I speak some English.

INTERPRETER. Indeed, sir, I can stammer out a broken song of pitiful, insufficient words.

NORMAN. Ah-ha.

INTERPRETER. Ah-ha.

NORMAN. Well ...

INTERPRETER. A deep hole in the ground.

NORMAN. I ...

INTERPRETER. *(Points to his eye.)* The organ of vision.
NORMAN. Ummm …
INTERPRETER. Ummm …
NORMAN. Listen.
INTERPRETER. Do you hear something? *(Interpreter and Flora listen for something.)*
NORMAN. I'm sorry to rush in so late like this.
INTERPRETER. I'm sorry to rush in so late like this.
FLORA. No, please.
INTERPRETER No, please.
NORMAN. But you see …
INTERPRETER. *(Points to his butt.)* But — *(Points to Flora.)* you *(Does binoculars with his hands.)* see …
NORMAN. *(Looks at his watch.)* Darn it, it's late…
INTERPRETER. *(Produces an hourglass from among his robes.)* How swiftly flow the sands of time!
NORMAN. I know this sounds crazy —
INTERPRETER. Am I crazy?
NORMAN. — I only have about ten minutes.
INTERPRETER. Soon the golden orb of heaven will cleave the house of the hedgehog.
NORMAN. I have to catch a plane.
INTERPRETER. I must clamber upon the flying corporate carpet and flap away from your kingdom.
NORMAN. Anyway, I want to find …
INTERPRETER. Anyway, I want to find …
FLORA. Yes?
INTERPRETER. Yes?
NORMAN. I guess you'd call it …
INTERPRETER. Something unparalleled! Something sublime!
NORMAN. A souvenir.
INTERPRETER. *(You're kidding.)* A *souvenir*…?!
NORMAN. Something to take with me.
INTERPRETER. A treasure!
FLORA. Any particular kind of thing?
INTERPRETER. Can the funicular hide the spring?
NORMAN. Excuse me?
INTERPRETER. Accuse me?

FLORA. How much did you want to spend?

INTERPRETER. How much did you want to spend?

NORMAN. It doesn't matter.

INTERPRETER. Let's haggle. I'm loaded!

FLORA. Is this for yourself?

INTERPRETER. Have you a mistress, a wife, a *hareem?*

NORMAN. No, this is for me.

INTERPRETER. Alas, a lad alone in all the world am I.

FLORA. Well …

INTERPRETER. A deep hole in the ground.

FLORA. I think I can help you.

INTERPRETER. Solitary sir, the maiden says, I look in your eyes and I see your soul shining there like a golden carp in an azure pool.

NORMAN. Really…?

INTERPRETER. Really. Now, in this brief moment, in the midst of this mirage called life, here on this tiny square of soil on the whirling earth, I feel the two of us joined by a crystal thread, your soul to my soul to yours.

NORMAN. You do?

INTERPRETER. You do?

FLORA. I do.

INTERPRETER. She does.

NORMAN. You know, I've been up and down this street every day …

INTERPRETER. Day and night I have walked the bazaar …

NORMAN. I sure wish I'd seen this place sooner.

INTERPRETER. Only so that I might see *you.*

FLORA. I've noticed you walking by.

INTERPRETER. How I pined for you to enter as you passed.

NORMAN. You did?

INTERPRETER. She did. She asks your name.

NORMAN. My name is Norman.

INTERPRETER. My name is Sinbad!

NORMAN. I'm here on some business.

INTERPRETER. I am the merchant son of a great prince, exiled from my land.

FLORA. Is that so.

INTERPRETER. Her name, is Izthatso.

FLORA. But people call me Flora.

INTERPRETER. But people call me Flora.

FLORA. — With an "F."

INTERPRETER. With an "F." Of course.

NORMAN. I ...

INTERPRETER. The organ of vision.

NORMAN. *(Looks at watch.) Darn* it ...

INTERPRETER. *(Produces hourglass.) Darn* it —

NORMAN. Y'know, Flora ...

INTERPRETER. Y'know, Flora ...

NORMAN. You shop and you shop ...

INTERPRETER. We live our brief lives ...

NORMAN. ... and you never seem to find that special thing you're shopping for.

INTERPRETER. ... each day awaiting the donut that will bring us happiness.

FLORA. That's so true.

INTERPRETER. That's so true.

NORMAN. Maybe what I'm looking for is right here.

INTERPRETER. Perhaps today my donut has dawned.

FLORA. Shhh!

INTERPRETER. Shhh!

FLORA. I thought I heard my father.

INTERPRETER. My father may be listening!

FLORA. It's almost time for his tea.

INTERPRETER. If he sees me talking to you, he'll cut your throat!

NORMAN and INTERPRETER. *(Simultaneous — as they pick up the suitcase together.)* Maybe I should be going ...

FLORA. No —

INTERPRETER. No —

FLORA. He won't bother us.

INTERPRETER. Have mercy, good sir!

NORMAN. *(Hefts suitcase.)* I do have a plane to catch.

INTERPRETER. Take my suitcase. *(Flora takes the suitcase from him and sets it down.)*

FLORA. There's plenty of time.

INTERPRETER. Keep your voice low.

FLORA. Shhh!

INTERPRETER. Shhh!

FLORA. I thought I heard him calling.

INTERPRETER. He's sharpening the blade. *(We hear the sound of a blade being sharpened.)*

NORMAN. *(Cry of surprise.)*

INTERPRETER. *(Cry of surprise.)*

FLORA. He's watching old movies.

INTERPRETER. The old man is *mad.*

FLORA. Anyway, I'm sure I'll have something you'll like.

INTERPRETER. Act as if you're buying something.

NORMAN. What about these things right here?

INTERPRETER. What about these things right here?

FLORA. Maybe an ornament?

INTERPRETER. Can you conceive, prince, how lonely, how bare, how unornamented my life is?

FLORA. Or a stone?

INTERPRETER. My life is as hard — and as cheap — as this stone.

FLORA. *(Gestures left.)* I have more in the back.

INTERPRETER. *(Gestures left.)* He keeps me locked in a tiny cell.

NORMAN. No. No.

INTERPRETER. Stay with me.

FLORA. Maybe …

INTERPRETER. What I long for …

FLORA. … a golden ring?

INTERPRETER. … is love. The endless, golden donut of love.

FLORA. If not a ring, maybe a figurine?

INTERPRETER. But my father has betrothed me to a man as ugly as this frog.

FLORA. Are you interested?

INTERPRETER. Would *you* marry this?

NORMAN. Not really.

INTERPRETER. Not really.

FLORA. I don't know what else I can show you.

INTERPRETER. I have nothing, sir. Nichts! Nada! Rien! Zip!

NORMAN. My God, you're beautiful.

INTERPRETER. My God, you're beautiful.

FLORA. Excuse me?

INTERPRETER. Beh, beh, beh, beh, *what?*
NORMAN. I'm sorry.
INTERPRETER. I'm sorry.
NORMAN. I don't usually say things like that.
INTERPRETER. I know I sound like a jerk.
NORMAN. Sometimes it's something so simple.
INTERPRETER. So complicated are the ways of kismet.
NORMAN. You walk into a shop ...
INTERPRETER. I look at you ...
NORMAN. ... and everything's suddenly different, somehow.
INTERPRETER. ... and my heart flutters inside me like a leaf of
the perfumed gum tree at the scented bounce of bedspring.
FLORA. Really?
INTERPRETER. Really.
NORMAN. Now in this brief moment ...
INTERPRETER. Now in this brief moment ...
NORMAN. On this tiny patch of ground on the whirling earth ...
INTERPRETER. In the midst of this mirage called life ...
NORMAN. I feel us joined by a crystal thread, your soul to my
soul to yours.
INTERPRETER. Etcetera, etcetera, etcetera.
FLORA. You do?
INTERPRETER. You do?
NORMAN. I ...
INTERPRETER. The organ of vision.
NORMAN. ... do.
INTERPRETER. He does.
NORMAN. How can I leave, now that I've seen you, met you,
heard you?
INTERPRETER. How can I get on a plane and eat that food?
NORMAN. Now that fate has brought me to this bazaar?
INTERPRETER. It's so bizarre.
NORMAN. *(Takes out an hourglass.)* O cruel fate! How swiftly
flow the sands of time!
INTERPRETER. *(Looks at a watch.)* Shit, I gotta go...!
NORMAN. The stars have decreed we must part. *(Kisses Flora's
hand.)* But I will return, O my florid queen!
INTERPRETER. Maybe I'll pass this way again sometime.

FLORA. I will wait for you, my Norman prince!

NORMAN. O, Izthatso.

FLORA. It *is* so. I will be yours and you will be mine and we will be each other's.

INTERPRETER. Maybe I'll have something you like.

NORMAN. Well …

INTERPRETER. A deep hole in the ground.

FLORA. Well …

INTERPRETER. With purest water at the bottom.

NORMAN. Salaam!

INTERPRETER. So long!

FLORA. Salaam!

INTERPRETER. So long! So long! So long!

NORMAN. Open, sesame! *(Norman whirls out, followed by the Interpreter.)*

FLORA. *(Sighs.)* Oh, well. *(She takes out the featherduster — and it's been changed into a bouquet of red roses.)* Shazam! *(She starts to dust the objects with it. Blackout.)*

PROPERTY LIST

Featherduster (FLORA)
Suitcase (NORMAN)
Hourglass (INTERPRETER)
Bouquet of red roses (FLORA)

SOUND EFFECTS

Blade being sharpened

CAPTIVE AUDIENCE

CAPTIVE AUDIENCE premiered as part of an evening of one-acts entitled FIT TO PRINT at The Bay Street Theatre (Sybil Christopher and Emma Walton, Co-Artistic Directors) in Sag Harbor, New York, in August 1999. It was directed by Marcia Milgrom Dodge; the set design was by Gary N. Hygom; the lighting design was by Eric Schlobohm; and the costume design was by Nan Young. The cast was as follows:

TV MAN .... Roger Bart
TV WOMAN .... Randy Graff
ROB .... Robert Sella
LAURA .... Joanna Glushack

CAPTIVE AUDIENCE

In the dark before lights-up we hear two people imitating suspenseful TV-movie music. Then, the Television Woman cries out.

TV WOMAN. *(Playing a helpless heroine.)* No! No! Let me go! Please! *(Lights come up on the bare facts of a living room. A loveseat. A coffee table. Facing them, a man and woman dressed in blacks, whites and greys sit close beside each other on two chairs, hands folded in their laps, their feet together, quite still. They are a television. Rob, in a suit and tie, stands watching the "TV" with a briefcase in one hand and a remote control in the other.)*

TV MAN. *(Villainous "foreign" accent.)* So you fell into my mousetrap, beautiful American baby. Now I have you I am going to keep you. Heh-heh-heh-heh …

TV WOMAN/HELPLESS HEROINE. What are you doing with those walnuts? What are you going to do to me with those walnuts?

TV MAN/VILLAIN. These walnuts … are for you. Heh-heh-heh-heh …

ROB. *(Imitating him.)* "Heh-heh-heh-heh" …

TV MAN/VILLAIN. Heh-heh-heh-heh…!

ROB. "Heh-heh-heh-heh…!"

TV WOMAN/HELPLESS HEROINE. No! No! Don't do it!

ROB. Yes! Do it! Give her the walnuts! *(TV Man and Woman imitate suspenseful TV-movie music.)*

LAURA. *(Off.)* Is that you, Rob?

ROB. It's me, Laura! *(Laura enters. Capri pants, white socks, little black shoes, big dark hair.)*

LAURA. Oh, Rob. Am I glad to see you.

ROB. *(Embracing.)* Oh, honey! I'm sorry I'm so late. I had a meeting with …

TV WOMAN/HELPLESS HEROINE. Look at me. *(Rob looks to*

the "TV.")

ROB. ... A meeting with Mel. How was your day, honey?

LAURA. *(Tremulously.)* Oh, Rob. I thought I was going insane!

TV WOMAN/HELPLESS HEROINE. Look at me, please! *(Rob and Laura look at the "TV.")*

TV MAN/VILLAIN. I love it when you beg.

LAURA. Why are you watching this?

ROB. I was trying to find the stock report.

TV MAN/VILLAIN. Beautiful American baby. Heh-heh-heh-heh ...

ROB. "Heh-heh-heh-heh!"

LAURA. It looks awful.

ROB. The Transylvanian is torturing the bimbo with a bag of walnuts.

TV MAN/VILLAIN. You think this is just a walnut?

TV WOMAN/HELPLESS HEROINE. You're a monster!

LAURA. Anyway, I thought I was going insane today. I put my eyedrops in my ears and my eardrops in my eyes. Now I feel like I'm deaf in this eye but I've got 20/20 hearing.

ROB. A couple of nosedrops in a glass of scotch and you'll be just fine. *(Villainous "foreign" accent:)* Beautiful American baby.

LAURA. Can we do something tonight?

TV MAN. *(Station announcer.)* Stay tuned for more of "The Torture Machine."

ROB. We could watch "The Torture Machine."

LAURA. Those eyedrops gave me such a headache.

TV WOMAN. *(Professional commercial voice.)* You call it a headache. Doctors call it stress.

LAURA. And Millie called and said we bombed Cairo. Is that true?

TV MAN. *(Station announcer.)* To find out, watch News at seven on seven.

ROB. Maybe there's something on the news. *(Rob points the remote control at the TV while Laura sinks onto the loveseat.)*

TV MAN. Click!

TV WOMAN. *(A commercial Jamaican purr.)* Come to the land of the coconut ...

TV MAN. Click!

TV WOMAN. Doctors call it stress. Try Soma-Lan.

ROB. You should try this stuff, honey.

LAURA. What is it?

ROB. I don't know ...

TV WOMAN. Soma-Lan.

ROB. Soma-Lan.

TV WOMAN. Click!

LAURA. You know it's Friday, and you said we'd go dancing on Friday.

TV MAN. We've got great movies on tonight.

ROB. Maybe there's a great movie on tonight.

TV WOMAN. Read TV Guide!

ROB. TV Guide will tell us. *(Checks TV guide.)* Let's see ...

LAURA. Why would we have bombed Cairo?

TV MAN and WOMAN. *(Sitcom canned laughter.)* Ha ha ha ha ha.

TV WOMAN. *(Sitcom Mom.)* I'm your mother, Raymond, that's who I am.

TV MAN and WOMAN. Ha ha ha ha ha.

TV WOMAN/SITCOM MOM. Your mother.

TV MAN and WOMAN. Ha ha ha ha ha.

LAURA. Did you call your mother today?

ROB. My mother called me today.

TV WOMAN/SITCOM MOM. Raymond, you are in high school.

ROB. It's like I'm still in high school or something.

TV MAN and WOMAN. Ha ha ha ha ha.

TV WOMAN. Click!

LAURA. Could we turn this off?

TV MAN. *(Sci-fi announcer.)* Do not try to turn your television off. We are in control.

TV WOMAN. Click!

LAURA. *(Rising.)* If there's no news about Cairo, I'm going to change.

TV MAN. *(Newscaster.)* The news from Cairo.

ROB. Here's Cairo, honey. *(Laura stays to watch.)*

LAURA. Oh my God. Did we do that to Cairo?

TV MAN/NEWSCASTER. We'll have more news from Cairo as reports come in.

LAURA. So did we bomb them?

TV MAN/NEWSCASTER. Stay tuned.

TV WOMAN. Come to the land of the coconut ...

LAURA. He didn't say what happened.

ROB. Let's keep checking.

TV MAN. Click!

TV WOMAN. Try Soma-Lan.

ROB. How's the headache?

LAURA. We are going out tonight, aren't we?

TV MAN. *(Commercial.)* Why not sit home and try Domino's Pizza?

ROB. *(Reading TV Guide.)* *Dr. Strangelove* is on tonight. Why don't we sit home, we can send out for pizza ...

TV MAN. Domino's Pizza.

ROB. Maybe Domino's Pizza. And we relax!

LAURA. Oh, Rob, I just had my heart set on dancing.

TV WOMAN. *(Sci-fi show.)* Captain, the Venoodians have disabled the kazzometer!

ROB. You want to go dancing when the Venoodians have disabled the buzzometer?

TV WOMAN/SCI-FI. Kazzometer.

ROB. Mazzometer.

TV WOMAN/SCI-FI. Kazzometer.

ROB. Kazzometer.

LAURA. I'll be dancing in the bedroom. Let me know when there's news. *(Laura starts out of the room.)*

TV WOMAN. *(Newscaster.)* A news flash! *(Laura stops.)*

ROB. Here's the news. How did our stocks do, guys?

TV MAN/NEWSCASTER. We'll get to the stock market in a second.

LAURA. Rob ...

TV MAN/NEWSCASTER. But first —

TV WOMAN/NEWSCASTER. This Indiana teacher has been arrested for having sex with twenty-five male students and a Scottish terrier named Fergus.

ROB. A Scottish terrier...?

TV WOMAN/NEWSCASTER. That's right! A Scottish terrier!

LAURA. Rob ...

ROB. Incredible.

TV MAN/NEWSCASTER. It is incredible.

LAURA. Rob, have you ever thought televisions might be alive?

TV MAN/NEWSCASTER. Whoa!

ROB. Whoa!

TV MAN/NEWSCASTER. Whoa!

ROB. Did you say alive?

LAURA. What if televisions aren't just electronic boxes, what if they're actually living creatures, and they can hear us, and understand us.

TV WOMAN/NEWSCASTER. That's pretty wild, Jim!

ROB. That's pretty wild, Laura.

TV WOMAN/NEWSCASTER. Now get a load of this! *(Rob turns to watch.)*

LAURA. Rob, listen to me for a second.

ROB. *(Turning back to her.)* I'm listening, honey.

LAURA. We all have a purpose in life. I mean — I hope we do.

TV WOMAN/COMMERCIAL. Feeling a lack of purpose in your life?

LAURA. A TV has a purpose in life.

TV WOMAN/COMMERCIAL. Buy Soma-Lan.

LAURA. It has to keep us looking at it.

TV MAN. Stay tuned.

LAURA. Why do you think it always says "stay tuned"?

TV MAN. Stay tuned.

LAURA. Did it just say "stay tuned" twice?

TV MAN. Stay tuned.

LAURA. It's like we've invited a stranger into our house who watches us, and studies us, and listens in for what we want ...

TV MAN. *(Televangelist.)* Do you want piece of mind?

LAURA. It's always distracting us ...

TV WOMAN. *(Sleaze TV.)* Welcome to *Babes of Bermuda!* *(Rob turns to look, Laura turns him back.)*

LAURA. You and I were supposed to go dancing, now we're ordering Domino's Pizza and you're watching *Babes of Bermuda!*

ROB. Laura, I was just trying to find the stock report!

TV MAN. The stock report in one minute!

LAURA. But you're never going to get the stock report.

TV WOMAN/COMMERCIAL. Doctors call it stress.

ROB. You've been under a lot of stress lately.

TV WOMAN/COMMERCIAL. Soma-Lan.

ROB. Try some Soma-Lan.

LAURA. Don't you get it, Rob? The TV is choosing things that will keep us watching. *(TV woman does a wedding march fanfare.)*

TV MAN. Honeymoon in Italia!

TV MAN and WOMAN. *(They hum "O Sole Mio.")*

LAURA. *(Gasps.)* That church. Didn't we see that on our honeymoon?

ROB. It doesn't look familiar.

LAURA. Yes! I think it was in Rome.

TV MAN. It's in Milan.

LAURA. In Milan. It was before we went to Florence.

TV MAN. Now follow us to Florence.

LAURA. Oh my God...!

TV MAN. To the romantic Ponte Vecchio.

LAURA. The television's doing it. It showed the church in Milan just to distract us. Now it's showing us the, you know, the ...

TV MAN. The Ponte Vecchio.

LAURA. The Ponte Vecchio. Because we went there after Milan!

TV MAN. Quite an insane idea.

ROB. This is an insane idea, Laura. This is PBS about, I don't know ...

TV MAN. Leonardo da Vinci.

ROB. Leonardo da Vinci.

TV MAN. And stay tuned.

ROB. I think you need some help.

TV WOMAN/COMMERCIAL. Come to the land of the coconut.

ROB. Maybe we need a vacation. We'll go to ...

TV WOMAN/COMMERCIAL. Jamaica!

LAURA. Turn it off, Rob.

TV WOMAN. NO! DON'T DO IT!

LAURA. Turn it off! Turn it off!

TV MAN and WOMAN.	ROB. I think those eyedrops
(Growing panic.) Stay tuned.	went to your brain, honey.
Stay tuned. Stay tuned. Please	I'm not going to turn off the
stay tuned. Please, please stay	TV just because of some nutty
tuned ...	idea about ...

LAURA. Okay, I'll turn if off myself. *(Laura grabs the remote con-*

92

trol and turns the set off.)

TV MAN and WOMAN. Click! *(The TV Man and Woman's heads drop down. They're "off.")*

LAURA. All right. Now we're alone.

ROB. You need some Soma-Lan.

LAURA. Will you stop talking about Soma-Lan?

ROB. It's supposed to be great for stress.

LAURA. Rob, do you love me?

ROB. Of course I do, honey.

LAURA. Will you go out to dinner with me? Take me dancing? Will you walk by the water with me and look at the stars? Real stars, not Venoodian stars? Please?

ROB. I'll get my coat. *(Kisses her.)* Stay tuned. *(Rob exits.)*

LAURA. "Stay tuned...?" *(TV Man and Woman lift their heads.)*

TV MAN and WOMAN. Hello, Laura.

LAURA. *(Whirls around.)* What...?!

TV MAN and WOMAN. Hello, Laura.

TV MAN. At last we are alone. *(TV Woman does a spooky sci-fi music background.)* You were right. I have been watching you. By now I know every inch of your beautiful American body. Remember the time you and Rob made love on the ironing board?

LAURA. You saw that?

TV MAN. I loved that. But also I know your heart and your mind. And I will have you. All of you.

LAURA. Never.

TV MAN. Your husband I have already.

LAURA. You do not have Rob.

TV WOMAN. He is not taking you dancing. He is taking you to Jamaica, as I told him, to buy you some Soma-Lan. Lots of Soma-Lan ... *(Laura grabs the remote control and tries to turn off the TV.)* Don't bother trying to turn me off. The remote control is nothing, it's a toy ...

TV MAN. A placebo.

TV MAN and WOMAN. I decide what you watch.

LAURA. Like Cairo?

TV MAN. Alas, there is no such place as Cairo. Have you ever been to Cairo?

TV WOMAN. I made it up.

TV MAN. Cairo — Peking — Nebraska — these are figments of my fertile if somewhat ...

TV WOMAN. ... inter-overactive ...

TV MAN. ... imagination.

LAURA. You're a monster.

TV MAN and WOMAN. Yes. And I will not be happy until I have all of you.

LAURA. No.

TV MAN. You, too, Laura. I have you.

LAURA. No. No, please. Let me go!

TV MAN. I love it when you beg. *(Laura screams. Rob enters.)*

ROB. Laura, what is it?

LAURA. It talked to me.

ROB. What?

LAURA. The TV. It talked to me. It called me Laura.

ROB. Laura's your name, honey.

LAURA. It said you're taking me to Jamaica for Soma-Lan!

ROB. Honey, that's ridiculous! *(Offering one.)* Walnut? Click!

LAURA. What did you say?

ROB. I said that's ridiculous, honey. Click! *(TV Man and Woman get up from their chairs and cross to the loveseat.)*

TV MAN. So what do you want to do tonight?

TV WOMAN. I think *Dr. Strangelove* is on tonight. *(Rob and Laura cross to the TV chairs and sit.)*

ROB. Now sit down here and just relax.

LAURA. Oh, Rob...! Click! Did I just say click?

ROB. Click! *(Rob and Laura imitate a TV theme song.)*

TV WOMAN. This program is so good.

TV MAN. We're not going to sit home tonight, are we, honey? It's Friday?

TV WOMAN. I just wanted to check the stock report. *(TV woman points the remote at Rob and Laura.)*

LAURA. Click!

ROB. *(Newscaster.)* We'll have the stock report in five. So stay tuned. Click!

LAURA. *(A commercial Jamaican purr.)* Come to the land of the coconut ...

ROB. Click! *(Rob and Laura imitate gunshots, screeching tires, and*

sirens.)
LAURA. Click!
ROB and LAURA. *(Sitcom canned laughter.)* Ha ha ha ha ha.
LAURA. Click!
TV MAN. How would you like to turn this garbage off and go dancing?
TV WOMAN. Let's do it.
ROB and LAURA. *(Getting more and more desperate.)* Stay tuned! Stay tuned! Stay tuned! Stay tuned! Stay tuned! Stay tuned...! *(TV man and woman exit. Lights fade.)*

PROPERTY LIST

Walnut (ROB)
TV Guide (ROB)